World Civilizations and Cultures

BY
DON BLATTNER

COPYRIGHT © 2000 Mark Twain Media, Inc.

ISBN   10-digit: 1-58037-146-9
          13-digit: 978-1-58037-146-9

Printing No. CD-1367

Mark Twain Media, Inc., Publishers
Distributed by Carson-Dellosa Publishing LLC

Visit us at www.carsondellosa.com

Table of Contents

Table of Contents

Introduction

While homo sapiens—humans—have been around for a couple hundred thousand years, for most of their history they were not considered "civilized." Humans originally lived in small groups and gathered nuts and berries and hunted in order to survive. Many were nomadic. That is, they moved from one place to another. They may have moved to follow herds of animals, or they may have had to search for new sources of plants, nuts, and berries. Overpopulation may have diminished the food source, or natural disasters such as fire, drought, or flood may have made moving necessary.

The Ice Age also caused humans to relocate. Huge populations had to move to warmer climates in order to survive. As much of the earth's surface water became ice, the level of the seas fell, making it easier for people to move from one continent to another. Eventually humans inhabited what is now Africa, Asia, Europe, Australia, and North and South America.

Better tools enabled people to build better shelters, and improved weapons allowed humans to become more efficient hunters, so they did not need to move around as much. Settlements sprang up, and many groups began to farm or grow their own food rather than hunt for it. Improved agricultural techniques eventually made it possible for humans to produce more food than they could consume. This allowed them to trade, build, create monuments, and invent new tools and weapons.

When people established cities, civilizations began to develop. This happened about 5,000 years ago. Culture, political and social development, and technological achievement are all characteristics of a civilization. Other characteristics include the invention of writing, mathematics, improved agricultural practices, sophisticated architecture, and trade.

This book follows the development of civilizations from their primitive beginnings in the Fertile Crescent over 5,000 years ago to more recent civilizations. It will not only examine many important civilizations and describe them in detail, but it will also highlight the achievements each civilization has contributed to our present life.

This book will also point out how cultures borrowed from previous cultures, adopting those elements they liked while rejecting those elements they didn't. This refining process, repeated many times, has given us the world we live in today. Perhaps Sir Isaac Newton, one of the greatest scientific geniuses of all time, made the point best when he said, "If I have seen further, it is because I have stood on the shoulders of giants." He was making the point that every inventor, scientist, philosopher, and artist is able to build or add to the inventions and accomplishments of those who have gone before. Many times these accomplishments can be traced to one man. Others are traced back to groups of people or to a civilization. The accomplishments of past civilizations have shaped the world we live in today.

For example, I am able to write this book because of the accomplishments of many civilizations. The Sumerians invented writing and mathematics, the Chinese invented paper, and the Phoenicians invented the alphabet. Each of these monumental inventions makes it possible for me to communicate with countless teachers and students.

One final note. It must be emphasized that when studying one civilization or culture at a time, students should be reminded that other civilizations and cultures were thriving simultaneously. One civilization did not abruptly end and another dramatically begin. For example, while the Assyrians were thriving, so were the Etruscans, Greeks, Phoenicians, and others.

The Fertile Crescent

The term "**Fertile Crescent**" refers to an area in the Middle East where the earliest known civilizations of the world began. The area got its name because the soil is fertile and the region is shaped like a crescent. Like a huge arch, the Fertile Crescent covers an area from the Persian Gulf through the Tigris and Euphrates River valleys and along the Mediterranean Sea. Some people refer to the eastern part of the Fertile Crescent as Mesopotamia. The western part of the Fertile Crescent is sometimes referred to as the Mediterranean section.

The Fertile Crescent was an ideal place for nomadic people to settle, build cities, and eventually develop civilizations. Sheep, goats, and various kinds of grains were found in abundance in the wild. With a permanent food source, there was no need to move around to find food. It was easier to grow crops in the rich soil and to raise animals for food. People living in the Fertile Crescent were able to grow more crops than they could eat and raise more animals than they needed, so they could trade the excess crops and animals with others. As trading increased, the population grew, and the people needed to develop laws, keep records, and invent ways to deal with their new way of life. There was a need for a written language, mathematics, laws, medicine, agriculture, and other developments because of the many people living close to one another.

When humans changed their lifestyle from hunters and fishers to farmers about 5,000 years ago in the Fertile Crescent, the developments and inventions that came from this change helped to develop the world's first civilizations. These civilizations have affected world history tremendously, not only in social and business areas, but in religion as well. Many of the great religions that exist in the world today had their beginnings in the area known as the Fertile Crescent.

The Fertile Crescent was not only the home of the first civilizations, but also the area where many later civilizations were developed. Some of the civilizations that developed in the Fertile Crescent were the Assyrians, Sumerians, Canaanites, Philistines, Phoenicians/Carthaginians, Akkadians, Hittites, Babylonians, Egyptians, Israelites, and others.

Identifying Modern Countries in the Fertile Crescent

Using an atlas, identify the middle-eastern countries that exist in the areas in and around the Fertile Crescent on the map at right. The outlines of the countries are shown as dashed lines.

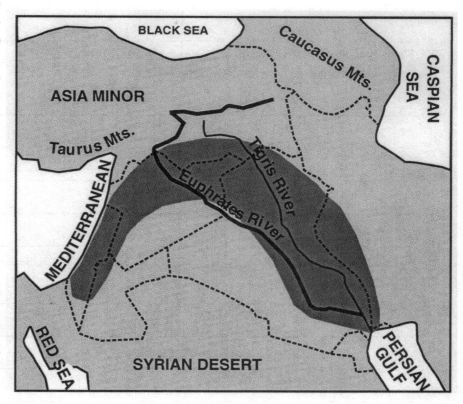

Name: _____ Date: _____

The Importance of the Fertile Crescent

Shown below are four statements relating to the importance of the Fertile Crescent. Read the statements below and then elaborate on them. To "elaborate" means you take the statement, explain its meaning, and add details or important information.

1. A fertile area allowed humans to settle in one place and develop civilizations.

   _____

   _____

   _____

   _____

2. A surplus of food meant that not everyone needed to hunt or farm.

   _____

   _____

   _____

   _____

3. People living in the Fertile Crescent were able to grow more food and raise more animals than they needed to eat.

   _____

   _____

   _____

   _____

4. The transition from hunting and farming to trading caused civilizations to develop.

   _____

   _____

   _____

Mesopotamia

Mesopotamia is a Greek word that means "between two rivers." The two rivers referred to are the Tigris and Euphrates Rivers. The Tigris and Euphrates Rivers begin in what is now Turkey, flow southeast, converge in the southeast in what is now Iraq, and empty into the Persian Gulf. The hot, dry climate of Mesopotamia was mixed with seasonal flooding, which made farming a challenge. Farmers in ancient Mesopotamia learned to deal with these problems by building levees to control the

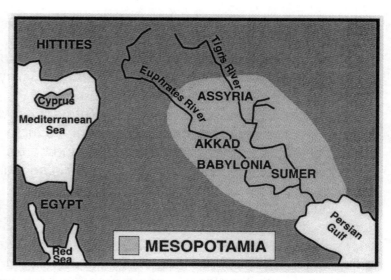

floods and developing irrigation systems in order to produce wheat, barley, sesame, and flax. They were also able to produce many different kinds of fruits and vegetables.

People talk about Mesopotamia as if it were a single civilization or culture. Actually, Mesopotamia was an area, not a civilization. It was composed of several independent city-states, each with its own religion, laws, language, and government. Many civilizations have existed in Mesopotamia, some of them at the same time. While one culture may have dominated a certain period, other cultures may have existed and were seeking to become independent. Some of the cultures that have existed in this area are Sumeria, Assyria, Babylon, and Iraq.

THE SUMERIANS AND THE AKKADIANS

The first group of people to inhabit Mesopotamia were the **Sumerians**. They originally lived in the mountains, but moved to the Plain of Shinar near the Persian Gulf to take advantage of the fertile soil. First, they drained the marshes and then controlled the Tigris and Euphrates Rivers by building levees and irrigation canals. As a result, the Sumerians had a stable food supply, and not everyone was needed to farm, hunt, or fish. Some Sumerians became tradesmen, merchants, soldiers, priests, government officials, and artisans. Their country was called **Sumer**.

The Sumerians are given credit for many inventions. One of the most important was the invention of a written language. Writing was invented so the Sumerians could keep records. Their writing was, of course, very simple. It was composed of pictures called **pictographs**. **Scribes**, who were professional writers, drew the pictures on clay tablets using a wedge-shaped instrument, or **stylus**. Over a period of time, the writing became more sophisticated. The pictures were replaced with shapes and lines. This type of writing is called **cunei-form**. Other inventions include the wheel,

SUMERIAN CIVILIZATION AT A GLANCE

WHERE: In the Middle East, between the Tigris and Euphrates Rivers

WHEN: 3500 B.C.–2000 B.C.

ACHIEVEMENTS:

- The world's first civilization where people lived together in a city-state
- Invented a written language
- Developed science and mathematics to a high degree; were able to divide the year and the circle into 360 parts
- Developed a twelve-month calendar based on lunar cycles
- Used the wheel and made vehicles
- Invented the plow and the sailboat

which was developed for making pottery, but was later used to make vehicles. They also invented the water clock, the twelve-month calendar, the plow, and the sailboat.

The Sumerians had a numbering system based on the number 60. We still use the Sumerian system today when measuring time. For example, sixty seconds make a minute and sixty minutes make an hour. Also, a circle has 360 degrees.

Between 3500 and 2000 B.C., the Sumerians were living in large villages. Eventually they became prosperous, and the villages developed into self-governing city-states. The buildings in these city-states were made of sun-dried mud bricks. The Sumerians used these mud bricks as building materials because there was no building stone and very little timber in Sumer, and the rivers were a great source for mud.

The buildings in Sumer were different from other civilizations, such as the Egyptians. Sumerians learned how to use a keystone to make arches. A **keystone** is a wedge-shaped stone in an arch that causes the arch to lock together. The doorways, gates, and other openings in buildings in the Sumerian cities had arches. Similar openings in Egyptian buildings were square.

Priests, wealthy citizens, and merchants had two-story houses. These houses had an open courtyard that all the rooms of the house opened into. There were smaller homes for others, also.

Religion was important to the Sumerians. At the center of each city-state was a temple that was surrounded by courts and public buildings. These temples were called **ziggurats**. Ziggurats were originally built on platforms, but eventually became temple-towers brightly decorated with glazed bricks. They were like huge pyramids with terraced sides that were flat on the top.

The Sumerians had many gods. They believed the gods spoke to them through their priests. Since the priests were representatives of the gods, they had a great deal of power in Sumer. When a priest commanded that something be done, the people believed the command was actually coming from one of their gods, and they obeyed. The ability to make important decisions and have people obey them elevated the status of priests. They became priest-kings and ruled large areas.

While Mesopotamia offered many advantages for settlement, such as rich soil, water, and game, there was one great disadvantage. The land did not provide any natural protection from invaders. Enemies could easily march into Sumer from almost any direction. This made Sumerians vulnerable to attack, not only from foreign armies, but from other Sumerian cities as well. Wars between Sumerian cities were common.

The importance of natural protection cannot be overstated. Compare the location of Egypt with Sumer, for example. Egypt is protected by a desert on both sides of the Nile River, which is difficult to navigate in some spots. Nations wanting to conquer Egypt would have a difficult time overcoming these natural barriers to launch an attack. Consequently, Egypt's culture grew rapidly. Sumer, on the other hand, did not have natural barriers. Sumerians not only had to worry about invading armies, but also about other groups of people who wanted to share the fertile soil of Mesopotamia.

One of the groups that moved into Sumeria was the **Akkadians**, who had been living on the Arabian peninsula. The Akkadians were a Semitic people. This means they spoke a **Semitic** language related to languages similar to Arabic and Hebrew. The Akkadians formed their own country where the Tigris and the Euphrates Rivers were close together. Their country was called **Akkad**. The Akkadians adopted much of the Sumerian culture. After many clashes between the Sumerians and the Akkadians, more Semites invaded Sumeria. The Sumerian culture was eventually absorbed by the invaders. This combined civilization lasted until about 1950 B.C. when the Amorites and the Elamites captured Ur, Mesopotamia's most important city.

Name: _____   Date: _____

Sumerian Civilization Quiz

Fill in the following sentences with the appropriate word or words.

1. Two famous rivers located in Mesopotamia are the _____ and _____ Rivers.

2. Farmers in ancient Mesopotamia learned to deal with flooding by developing _____ _____.

3. Ziggurats were originally built on platforms, but eventually became _____.

4. Some of the cultures that have existed in _____ were Sumeria, Assyria, Babylon, and Iraq.

5. The first group of people to inhabit Mesopotamia was called _____.

6. The name of the country of the first inhabitants of Mesopotamia was _____.

7. Perhaps the most important Sumerian invention was a _____.

8. Mesopotamia is a Greek word that means _____.

9. Sumerian writing was originally composed of pictures, called _____.

10. _____ were professional writers.

11. Scribes drew the pictures on clay tablets using a wedge-shaped instrument, or _____.

12. Later Sumerian writing consisting of shapes and lines was called _____.

13. The Sumerians invented writing so that they could keep _____.

14. At the center of each Sumerian city-state was a temple called a _____.

15. Mesopotamia was composed of several independent _____ .

16. Ziggurats were like huge _____ with terraced sides that were flat on the top.

17. A _____ is a wedge-shaped stone in an arch that causes the arch to lock together.

18. The Sumerians believed that the gods spoke to them through their _____.

19. Sumerians learned how to use a keystone to make _____ .

20. Egypt is protected by a _____ on both sides of the Nile.

21. The priests were actually _____, and they ruled large areas.

22. Mesopotamia did not provide any natural _____ from invaders.

23. One of the groups that moved into Sumeria was the _____.

24. The Akkadians formed a country called _____ .

25. The Akkadians were a _____ people.

Babylonia

The Sumerians and Akkadians living in Mesopotamia became weaker and were conquered by the Amorites, a Semitic tribe from Syria. One Akkadian town that developed in approximately 1900 B.C. was the small town of Babylon, located by the Euphrates River. Babylon grew in size and importance, and eventually its ruler, King Hammurabi, conquered all of Mesopotamia. This kingdom came to be known as **Babylonia**.

The Babylonian culture was similar to the Sumerian culture, which had existed in Mesopotamia before the Babylonians arrived. In fact, many people refer to the Babylonians as just a later development of the Sumerian culture. This is why some historians credit Sumeria with some inventions and developments while other historians credit the same advances to Babylonia. This confusion is easy to understand. While the two civilizations existed at different times, they had many things in common. The Babylonians adopted the religion, literature, inventions, and practices of the Sumerians. Scholars and priests spoke the Sumerian language, although most Babylonians did not. While Babylonia borrowed heavily from the Sumerian culture, they did make one important contribution to the world. This contribution was a code of laws known as the ***Code of Hammurabi***.

Hammurabi was king of Babylonia from 1792 B.C. to 1750 B.C. He was a powerful leader with strong armies. Under his leadership, Babylon expanded by conquering other kingdoms. Hammurabi was not only an excellent military leader, he was an efficient administrator. While most ancient leaders considered only the comfort and pleasures of themselves and other noblemen, Hammurabi was also concerned with the lives of *all* of the people in his kingdom. He wanted everyone in his kingdom to have enough food, adequate housing, and to be treated fairly. In order to make sure that everyone was treated fairly, he had his scribes draw up a code of laws that are known as the *Code of Hammurabi*. The laws in the code were not completely original. They were taken, for the most part, from the written laws developed by the Sumerians. Hammurabi's code was a little different from the laws devised by the Sumerians, however. Hammurabi's code added the element of revenge. In Sumeria, most who committed a crime were fined. The *Code of Hammurabi* did not impose a fine on criminals, but substituted the ancient punishment of *"an eye for an eye, and a tooth for a tooth."* In other words, if someone did something bad to a person, in many cases, the court would do the same thing to the wrongdoer.

Some laws in the code seem very extreme and cruel. For example, if a son slapped his father, the son's hands would be cut off. If a man killed another man's son, then his son would be killed. While this may seem harsh by today's standards, it should be remembered that before the code was written and followed, punishment was often decided by priests and judges who imposed punishments even more harsh. Death was a common punishment for even the most minor offenses. So the philosophy of *"an eye for an eye, and a tooth for a tooth,"* was not meant to be cruel, but to be fair.

The Code did distinguish between classes of people. A person's punishment depended on who was wronged. For example, if a man put out the eye of another man, his eye would then be put out. But if he put out the eye of a freed man (a former slave), he would pay one gold mina. If

---

BABYLONIAN CIVILIZATION AT A GLANCE

WHERE: On the Euphrates River
WHEN: 2000–1155 B.C.
ACHIEVEMENTS:
- Devised a code of laws, known as the *Code of Hammurabi*, designed to protect the weak
- Studied astronomy
- Built beautiful buildings as well as the Gate of Ishtar and the Hanging Gardens of Babylon

he put out the eye of a man's slave, he would then have to pay one-half of the slave's value.

Law was not the only interest of the Babylonians. They studied astronomy and also believed in astrology. **Astronomy** is the study of the universe, including the movement of the stars and planets. **Astrology** is the belief that the positions and movements of the planets and stars can affect or predict life on Earth. While we separate these two areas today, the Babylonians did not.

The study of astronomy by the Babylonians was very advanced for its time. They not only watched the stars and heavens, they kept records of events, such as when an eclipse occurred. They were able to measure time by studying the movements of the celestial bodies. The priests used their knowledge of planets and the stars as part of their religion. The priests claimed that by studying the celestial bodies, they could tell the future. They were constantly looking at the skies, making horoscopes and predictions based on what they saw. A **horoscope** is a prediction of a person's future based on a diagram of the planets and stars at a given moment, such as birth.

About 1,000 years after the death of Hammurabi, another king came to power. His name was Nebuchadnezzar II. By this time, Babylon was part of the Chaldean Empire, which came to power after the Assyrian Empire was destroyed. Nebuchadnezzar ruled Babylon from 605 B.C. to 562 B.C., and under his leadership, Babylon grew. At this time, Babylon had two structures that were so impressive they were known throughout the civilized world. The first was the beautifully decorated wall surrounding Babylon. On top of the wall were towers for guards who could watch for approaching enemies. This wall was wide enough for a four-horse chariot to be driven on it. While the wall had several gates through which travelers could enter and leave the city, the most impressive was the Gate of Ishtar. **Ishtar** was a goddess, and the gate named in her honor was made of colorful glazed enamel bricks with pictures of animals. The gate was so beautiful that at one time it was considered as one of the Seven Wonders of the Ancient World. It was later replaced on the list by the Lighthouse at Alexandria.

The second structure built by Nebuchadnezzar that gained worldwide fame was the Hanging Gardens of Babylon. The Hanging Gardens is still considered one of the Seven Wonders of the Ancient World. Built to please Nebuchadnezzar's wife, Amytis, the Hanging Gardens was a building consisting of several terraces, one above the other. Each terrace was planted with trees and flowers from around the country. Pools and fountains were also built into the structure. In order for all of the plant life to thrive in this desert environment, the Babylonians developed an irrigation system to raise water from the Euphrates River to the Gardens. Exactly how this irrigation system worked is unknown, but later writers referred to the system as "water engines."

Nebuchadnezzar was succeeded by his son in 562 B.C. who was assassinated three years later. Within a few years, Babylon was invaded by the Persians, and Babylon became part of the Persian Empire.

The Hanging Gardens of Babylon

Name: _____   Date: _____

Babylonian Civilization Quiz

Fill in the following sentences with the appropriate word or words.

1. The priests used their knowledge of planets and the stars as part of their _____.

2. King Hammurabi had a code of laws that are known as the _____.

3. _____ is the study of the universe.

4. _____ is the belief that the positions and movement of the planets and stars can affect or predict life on Earth.

5. About 1,000 years after the death of Hammurabi, _____ came to power.

6. The most impressive gate in the Wall of Babylon was the _____.

7. Ishtar was a _____ .

8. The Hanging Gardens of Babylon were built to please Nebuchadnezzar's wife _____.

9. The Hanging Gardens is considered one of the _____.

10. Babylon was invaded by the _____, and Babylon became part of their empire.

11. Babylon was located by the _____ River.

12. Nebuchadnezzar ruled Babylon from _____ to _____ .

13. _____ was king of Babylonia from 1792 B.C. to 1750 B.C.

14. The _____ Empire came to power after the Assyrian Empire was destroyed.

15. The *Code of Hammurabi* did not impose a fine on criminals but substituted the ancient punishment of "an eye for an _____ , and a tooth for a _____."

16. Babylonians were able to measure time by studying the movements of _____ _____ .

17. The _____ were a Semitic tribe from Syria who conquered the Sumerians and the Akkadians.

18. Nebuchadnezzar was succeeded by his _____ in 562 B.C.

19. The *Code of Hammurabi* was a little different from those adopted from Sumeria. It added the element of _____ to the code.

20. Many people refer to the Babylonians as a later development of the _____ culture.

The Assyrians

Assyria was a civilization in Mesopotamia on the upper Tigris River. The civilization lasted many centuries, but was most prominent between 1600 B.C. and 612 B.C. Assyria had several advantages over Babylonia. Assyrians could farm without the elaborate irrigation that was needed in Babylonia. The land not only received water from the Tigris River and its tributaries, but it also received a moderate amount of rainfall annually. Also, Assyria had rocks and stones that could be used for building. Assyria had two disadvantages, however, compared to Babylonia. The Assyrian land was harder to cultivate, and they were often attacked by barbarians who raided their villages.

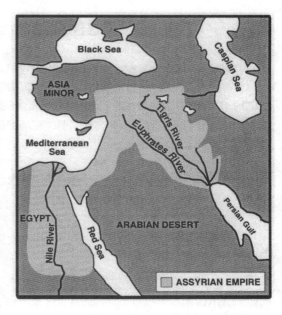

Assyrians were a Semitic-speaking people who arrived in Mesopotamia about 2000 B.C. Assyria was named after its original capital, Ashur. Ashur became part of the Mesopotamian empire but eventually gained its independence in about 1365 B.C. Assyrians developed a thriving trade in Anatolia (Asia Minor). Eventually, the Hittites drove the Assyrians out of Anatolia, and when the Babylonian Kingdom became stronger under the leadership of King Hammurabi, Assyrian power in Mesopotamia grew weaker. By 1550 B.C. Assyria became part of the Mitanni Kingdom. The notable achievement of the Mitanni Kingdom was that it introduced trained horses and chariots into this part of the world.

Gradually, Assyrian power grew and by 1100 B.C. it was strong enough to begin expanding. Assyria's method of expansion was very different from those of other civilizations. The Assyrians developed a **standing army**, which is composed of soldiers who choose the army as their career. When the soldiers are not fighting, they are still in the army training to fight. This was a revolutionary idea in this period. Other countries fought their wars with citizen-soldiers. A **citizen-soldier** fights a war, and after it is over, he returns home and resumes his life working at his former craft or career.

The Assyrian soldiers were fierce and cruel warriors. They had weapons made of iron rather than copper or bronze. They also had battering rams. They not only had foot soldiers, they had archers, chariots, and a cavalry. Whenever they captured enemies, they would either murder them or make them slaves.

Captured cities were plundered and looted. Once a city was conquered by the Assyrians, the citizens of the city were required to pay taxes and tribute to the Assyrians. The Assyrians built forts close to these cities, and a governor was appointed to administer each of these forts. The governor reported directly to the king by sending reports by messengers on horseback—the first mail delivery service.

However, the success of the Assyrians was also their undoing. Because their kingdom was so large, it was impossible to maintain. There were too few soldiers, so mercenaries were hired to serve in the army. A **mercenary** is a foreign soldier hired by another country to fight in its army. Eventually, the Assyrians were vanquished by the Medes, Chaldeans, and the Babylonians. The capital city of Nineveh was razed.

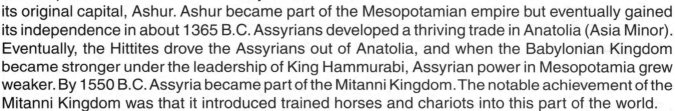

ASSYRIAN CIVILIZATION AT A GLANCE

WHERE: Northern Mesopotamia
WHEN: 1600 B.C.–612 B.C.
ACHIEVEMENTS:
- Created the first library
- Built a system of roads
- Ruled their extended kingdom with appointed governors
- First to develop a standing army
- Developed a mail service

Name: _____ Date: _____

Assyrian Civilization Synonyms

Shown below are several words used in the explanation of the Assyrian Civilization. Look at each word written in boldface type and then find the word or phrase at the right that has *almost* the same meaning. Words that have the same meaning are called synonyms. Circle the correct synonym, and then write a sentence using that synonym on the line below each group of words.

1. **civilization** A. country B. sane C. culture

_____

2. **irrigation** A. watered B. irritated C. farmed

_____

3. **cultivate** A. fix B. grow C. ask

_____

4. **tributaries** A. streams B. divisions C. banks

_____

5. **thriving** A. lingering B. dying C. prospering

_____

6. **moderate** A. reasonable B. excessive C. insufficient

_____

7. **warriors** A. soldiers B. Indians C. leaders

_____

8. **independent** A. dependent B. joyous C. self-sufficient

_____

9. **revolutionary** A. free B. circular C. radical

_____

10. **standing army** A. mercenaries B. inductees C. career soldiers

_____

11. **fort** A. army post B. home C. mess hall

_____

Name: _____ Date: _____

Assyrian Civilization Synonyms (continued)

12. **tribute**   A. payment   B. award   C. protest

_____

13. **governor**   A. assistant   B. lieutenant   C. commander

_____

14. **mercenaries**   A. hirelings   B. foreign   C. ethical

_____

15 **besiege**   A. surround   B. fight   C. betray

_____

16. **cavalry**   A. swordsmen   B. horse soldier   C. spearmints

_____

17. **chariot**   A. charity   B. carriage   C. horse

_____

18. **archers**   A. bowmen   B. masons   C. groomsmen

_____

19. **battering ram**   A. mammal   B. weapon   C. mascot

_____

20. **conquered**   A. lost   B. captured   C. prevailed

_____

21. **prominent**   A. outstanding   B. nice   C. overlooked

_____

22. **capital**   A. gymnasium   B. headquarters   C. arena

_____

23. **appointed**   A. designated   B. fired   C. hired

_____

Name: _____ Date: _____

Mesopotamia Crossword Puzzle Clues

Use the clues below to complete the crossword puzzle on page 13 about Mesopotamia.

ACROSS

1. Means "between two rivers"
3. A wedge-shaped instrument made of reed and used for writing
5. Mesopotamia's most important city
8. The writing system invented by the Sumerians; it literally means "wedge-shaped"
11. A Babylonian king
13. Raised areas of earth designed to hold back the floodwaters
17. One of two rivers that forms Mesopotamia
18. A forecast of a person's future, based on a diagram of the planets and stars at a given moment
22. The Hanging _____ was considered one of the Seven Wonders of the Ancient World.
23. The name we give to a priest who also ruled a city-state (hyphenated word)

DOWN

2. One of two rivers that forms Mesopotamia
3. The name given to a writer in ancient civilizations
4. The world's first civilization
6. Civilization founded by a group of Semitic people who moved to Sumeria and adopted the Sumerian culture
7. A collection of kingdoms under one powerful ruler
8. Not only the city, but the area surrounding the city (hyphenated word)
9. The Gate of _____ was the most impressive gate into Babylon.
10. The material used to make bricks
12. A system to artificially supply dry land with water
14. A Sumerian invention that made planting easier and faster
15. The study of space, stars, and planets
16. Hammurabi established a set of laws that are known as the _____ of Hammurabi.
19. Moist, sticky earth that can be shaped when wet but hardens when heated; it was used to make tablets in Sumeria
20. People who perform religious rites
21. A Sumerian temple

A Sumerian Ziggurat

Name: _____ Date: _____

Mesopotamia Crossword Puzzle

Use the clues on page 12 to complete the crossword puzzle below.

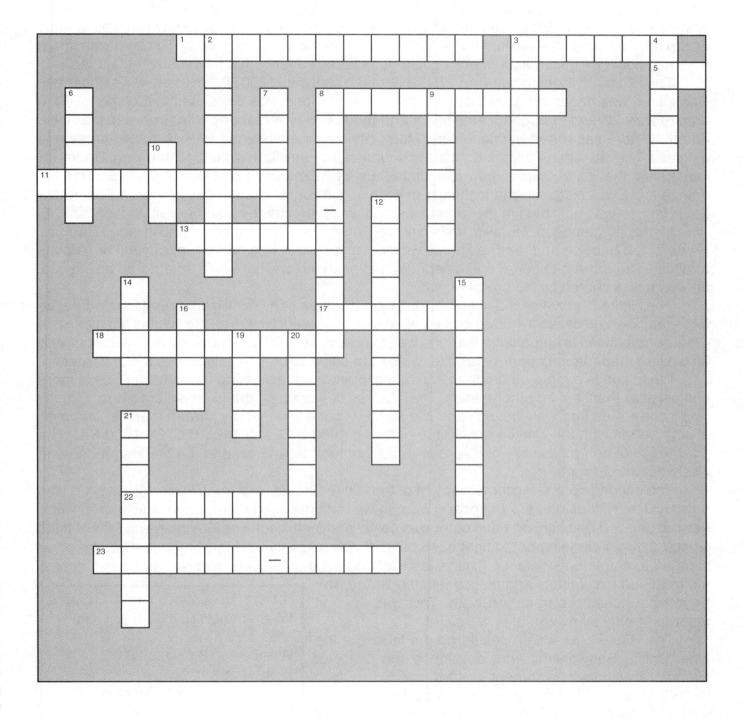

The Hittites

After Hammurabi died, Mesopotamia grew weak, and other civilizations, such as the **Hittites** who lived in central Turkey, were being established. The Hittites were originally migrant peasants who lived north of the Black Sea. About 2300 B.C. they moved into **Anatolia**, which was already occupied. Anatolia is the ancient name for Asia Minor, which is Turkey today. The land was rocky, but grain could be grown and animals could be raised. The land also held many metal ores.

The Hittite Civilization began in 1750 B.C. and lasted until 1200 B.C. In many ways, the Hittite Civilization was not as organized as some other civilizations. The city-states that comprised the empire were spread throughout Asia Minor and Syria. There were many miles between the cities, and they were separated by mountains. Many city-states maintained their own languages and religions. The city-states often fought among themselves until Labarnas became king. Under his leadership, the Hittite empire grew to include most of Turkey. His son, Hattusilis I, expanded the empire into Syria. Hattusilis made the city of Hattusa the capital of the Hittite Kingdom. For protection, Hattusa was built high in the mountains and was protected by a stone wall 26 feet thick.

Hattusilis' grandson, Mursilis, rose to power, strengthened the empire, and invaded Babylon. He defeated Babylon and returned home with loot and captives he had taken from the once-powerful city. The crowds cheered and celebrated his great victory, but when he entered his palace, he was assassinated by his brother-in-law.

The Hittite Civilization did not really originate a culture of its own. It borrowed from other cultures and in some cases slightly modified what was borrowed. However, the Hittites did make two great contributions to humankind. The first was the use of iron. Before the use of iron, weapons and tools were made from copper or bronze, which are soft and bend easily. Iron is much harder.

While iron is a more common metal than copper or tin, extracting the metal for use is more complicated than it is for other metals. The process of extracting ore is called **smelting**. Exactly when and where iron was first smelted is a mystery, but it is generally agreed that real iron metallurgy began with the Hittites some time between 1900 B.C. and 1400 B.C. By 1000 B.C., the knowledge of iron metallurgy had spread throughout the Near East and the Mediterranean and westward into Europe.

The second notable accomplishment of the Hittite Empire, occurring in the 1200s B.C., was a treaty. The Hittites and the Egyptians went to war against each other. Each side scored victories but decided that fighting each other was costly and inefficient. The Egyptians and the Hittites signed a treaty pledging not to fight each other. If one was attacked by someone else, the other pledged to come to its defense. The treaty was engraved on a silver plaque. The Hittites copied the treaty on clay tablets and placed it in the library. The Egyptians etched the treaty on walls. This was the first recorded treaty by two great powers.

The Hittite laws were considered the fairest of the time. Unlike Babylonians who developed the *Code of Hammurabi* where punishment was "an eye for an eye," the Hittite law tried to compensate the person who was wronged. According to Babylonian law, if a man injured another, the man who caused the injury would be injured the same way. In the Hittite civilization, however, he would have to pay a fine to the person he injured.

HITTITE CIVILIZATION AT A GLANCE

WHERE: Anatolia, the ancient name for Asia Minor

WHEN: 1750 B.C.–1200 B.C.

ACHIEVEMENTS:
- One of the first civilizations to use iron
- Signed peace treaties
- Established a set of laws considered the fairest of the time

---

Name: _____ Date: _____

Hittite Civilization Quiz

Shown below are a number of sentences. Some are true and some are false. If the sentence is true, write "true" in front of the sentence. If the sentence is false, write a term that could replace the word in bold type to make the sentence true.

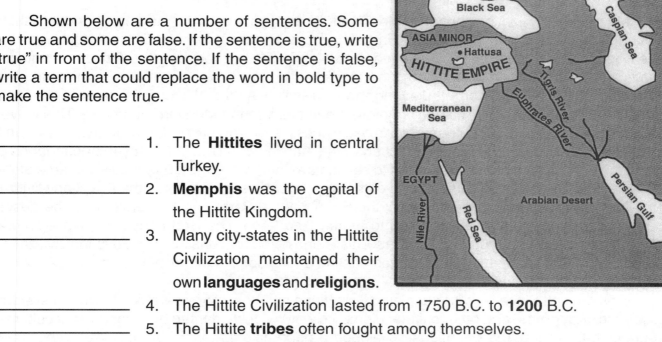

_____ 1. The **Hittites** lived in central Turkey.

_____ 2. **Memphis** was the capital of the Hittite Kingdom.

_____ 3. Many city-states in the Hittite Civilization maintained their own **languages** and **religions**.

_____ 4. The Hittite Civilization lasted from 1750 B.C. to **1200** B.C.

_____ 5. The Hittite **tribes** often fought among themselves.

_____ 6. Under **Alexander's** leadership, the Hittite empire grew to include most of Turkey.

_____ 7. Labarnas' son, Hattusilis I, expanded the Hittite Empire into **Africa**.

_____ 8. The Hittite Civilization did not really originate a **culture** of its own.

_____ 9. The Hittite laws were considered the **cruelest** of the time.

_____ 10. Before the use of iron, weapons and tools were made from **copper** or **bronze**.

_____ 11. The Hittites were not as **organized** as some other civilizations.

_____ 12. The Hittite law tried to **compensate** a person who was wronged.

_____ 13. The Hittites were originally migrant peasants who lived north of the **Netherlands**.

_____ 14. Anatolia is the ancient name for **Asia Major**.

_____ 15. The process of extracting ore is called **boiling**.

_____ 16. The Hittites were among the first to use **dental floss**.

_____ 17. The Hittites and the Egyptians made the first recorded **treaty** by two great civilizations.

_____ 18. Hattusa had a stone **tower** 26 feet thick.

_____ 19. **Mursilis** was assassinated by his brother-in-law.

_____ 20. Knowledge of **steel** metallurgy began with the Hittites.

Ancient Egypt

Many great civilizations began beside rivers. There was rich soil for farming, abundant fishing and hunting, and water for drinking and irrigating crops. Between July and October each year, the Nile River, located in northeast Africa, fed by rain and melting snow from the African mountains, floods and spills over its banks. During the water's swift descent down the mountains, the turbulent streams pick up soil and carry it down to the river valley. As the Nile surges towards the Delta Region, the water overflows its banks before it empties into the Mediterranean Sea. This leaves behind a layer of silt, rich in nutrients that make it possible to grow crops in this otherwise arid land.

This is the fertile land that people began to settle in 3300 B.C. Drawn by the abundance of food provided by the Nile, people began to settle, farm, and build cities. Eventually, the area along the Nile River became the home of one of the world's earliest civilizations, the Egyptian Civilization. The Egyptians called their country the Black Land, referring to the fertile soil. The desert surrounding their country was referred to as the Red Land. The Red Land provided a natural barrier that protected Egypt from invaders. This is one of the reasons that the Egyptian civilization lasted over 3,000 years. It was the longest-lasting civilization in history, and its influence was so powerful that it is still felt today.

Egyptian influence on other ancient civilizations has been considerable. Its writing system, called **hieroglyphics**, and other cultural elements were widely adapted by other ancient cultures. In addition to writing, the Egyptians developed a paper-like material from **papyrus** reed. They also used papyrus to make mats, ropes, toys, boats, and other items.

Egyptians were excellent architects, builders, craftsmen, and artisans. They built huge pyramids in which to bury their pharaohs. One pyramid, the Great Pyramid of Giza, was so large and magnificent it was listed as one of the Seven Wonders of the Ancient World. It is the only one of these wonders that still stands today. The Great Pyramid of Giza was built over 5,000 years ago without modern machines or tools. Over two and one-third million stone blocks, each weighing about two and one-half tons, were transported from a stone quarry on the other side of the Nile and built into a pyramid about as high as a 42-story skyscraper. All of this was done with manpower alone. Built near the Great Pyramid of Giza was the Sphinx, a huge stone sculpture of a creature with the face of a human and the body of a lion.

The Egyptians were superb engineers as well. They built canals, dams, and a reservoir to control the flood waters of the Nile. They even built a canal from the Nile to the Red Sea in order to improve trade.

Egyptians believed in life after death; a person's soul would continue to live as long as the body was preserved. The Egyptians practiced **mummification** of the dead. When someone died, their body was prepared in such a way that it would dry out and not decay. The bodies of the wealthy were wrapped in linen. Jewels and charms were inserted in the layers of linen in order to protect the deceased. The poor were generally buried naked in shallow graves.

Archaeology, history, and drama have made Egypt a subject of interest. Countless plays, books, movies, and even operas have been based on this ancient civilization.

EGYPTIAN CIVILIZATION AT A GLANCE

WHERE: Along the Nile River in northeast Africa

WHEN: 3100 B.C.–332 B.C.

ACHIEVEMENTS:

- Built the pyramids, the sphinx, canals, and temples
- Invented a calendar with 365 days
- Made a paper-like material from the papyrus plant
- Used a loom to weave cloth
- Invented a system of writing called hieroglyphics

Egypt's Three Kingdoms

The Egyptian Civilization is generally divided into three periods: the Old Kingdom, the Middle Kingdom, and the New Kingdom.

THE OLD KINGDOM

The first period of the Egyptian Civilization is called the Old Kingdom. It lasted from 3100 B.C. until 2040 B.C. Before 3400 B.C., Egypt was really two different kingdoms—Upper Egypt and Lower Egypt. These names are deceiving because if you look at a map of this ancient country, you will see that **Lower Egypt** was located at the top of the map in the northern delta where the river spreads out and empties into the Mediterranean Sea. **Upper Egypt** was located in the south, and would be found on the bottom of the map. This inconsistency is easy to understand since the Nile flows north, not south. It flows parallel to the Red Sea and eventually empties into the Mediterranean Sea.

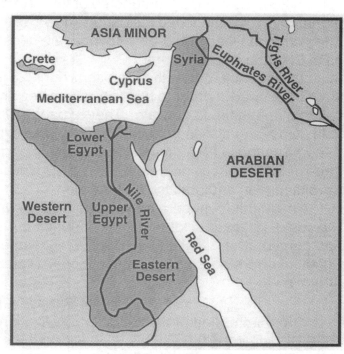

About 3100 B.C., King Menes, a king from the south, was credited with combining the Upper and Lower Kingdoms and uniting Egypt. Menes became the first pharaoh of Egypt. **Pharaoh** was the term given to the king or ruler in Egypt. Menes was the first king of the first dynasty of Egypt. Eventually there would be thirty dynasties to rule Egypt. A **dynasty** is a series of rulers from the same family or line.

It was during the Old Kingdom that many pyramids were built. One of the most important pyramids was the Great Pyramid of Giza. It was built as a tomb for the pharaoh Khufu. He is sometimes called Cheops.

During the Old Kingdom, pharaohs were considered gods. They owned the land and everything in the country. They could do anything they wanted and make any law they wanted to. This was called the "divine rights of kings."

Menes made Memphis the capital of Egypt. Since the country was so large, he could not rule it all by himself. He needed help. He assigned people he trusted to govern different sections of Egypt. These governors, or **nomarchs**, worked to be sure that all of the commands of the pharaoh were obeyed.

The Egyptian Kingdom was very large. Since the pharaoh lived in Memphis, and the nomarchs governed for the pharaoh in various parts of the kingdom, communication was important. In order to make communication more efficient, the Egyptians developed a written language called hieroglyphics. **Hieroglyphics** uses pictures of objects, such as animals or plants, to represent words. The Egyptian writers, or scribes, wrote their messages and kept records on a paper-like material that the Egyptians made from the papyrus reed.

About 2200 B.C., the nomarchs began to act more independently and obeyed the king less. Many broke away from Egypt, establishing their own provinces. Some of the nomarchs fought each other over territory. Eventually two separate kingdoms were established.

THE MIDDLE KINGDOM

In 2040 B.C., King Mentuhotep of the 11th dynasty reunited Egypt. He created a centralized monarchy, which launched the period known as the Middle Kingdom. He made Thebes his capital. The nomarchs lost power, and Egypt again became a centralized government. The pharaoh had all of the power in the country.

Things went well for the Egyptians during this time. Egypt became prosperous. New quarries were developed in order to build more temples and other structures. They built dams and a reservoir to manage the flood water. They expanded their kingdom south to Nubia. Egyptians brought gold, ivory, and slaves from Nubia. They also expanded trade during this period. The Egyptians traded with those living in the Middle East, along the Mediterranean, and in other locations. This trade brought peace and wealth to Egypt. Egyptians had time to create works of art, build temples, develop crafts, and practice their religion.

The Middle Kingdom ended when Egypt was conquered by the Hyksos from Canaan. The Hyksos were good soldiers and had superior weapons. The Hyksos had horse-drawn chariots and curved swords called scimitars, which were made of bronze. The wooden weapons of the Egyptians were no match for these modern weapons.

THE NEW KINGDOM

The third period of the Egyptian Civilization is called the New Kingdom, and it lasted from 1600 B.C. until 1100 B.C. This is considered the last great period in Egyptian history. You probably noticed that the Middle Kingdom ended about 1800 B.C. and the New Kingdom began about 1600 B.C. What happened to those 200 years in between? Did Egypt cease to exist? In a way it did. During this time, Egypt was conquered by the Hyksos, who had superior weapons. Eventually, the Egyptians began using these newer weapons as well and were able to win their country back from the Hyksos. Egypt was united once more, and the New Kingdom, sometimes called the Golden Age of Egypt or the Age of Empire, began.

Egyptian armies conquered Syria, Palestine, and the area west of the Euphrates River. Egypt became wealthy. Pharaoh Amenhotep IV forced the people to stop worshipping many gods and told them they should only worship one god, Aten, the sun god. He closed the temples of other gods and had workmen remove the plural word "gods" from buildings and from other structures. He was so devoted to the god Aten, he even changed his own name to Akhenate, which means "spirit of Aten." He created a new capital named Akhetaton, devoted to the god. When Akhenate died, Pharaoh Tutankhamen (Tut) restored the old gods and made Thebes the capital again.

Beginning in 1070 B.C., the Egyptian Empire began to decline. There was a civil war. Egypt also had to defend itself from many different invasions over these years. Egyptians fought the Hittites, the Lybians, the Nubians, and the "sea peoples," invaders from somewhere in the Mediterranean. Over a period of time, the Egyptians were invaded by the Assyrians in 671 B.C., the Persians in 525 B.C., Alexander the Great in 332 B.C., and the Romans in 32 B.C.

Artifact from King Tut's Tomb

Name: _____ Date: _____

Egyptian Civilization Crossword Puzzle

Use the clues below to complete the crossword puzzle about the Egyptian Civilization.

ACROSS

3. Governors assigned to carry out the pharaoh's commands
8. A body preserved by drying
10. The Nile River empties into this sea.
11. The name given to the king or ruler of Egypt
12. The shortened name of the pharaoh who succeeded Amenhotep IV
13. The fine sediment left behind when a flood recedes
14. Location of the pyramid that is considered one of the Seven Wonders of the Ancient World
15. Curved swords used by the Hyksos

DOWN

1. A kind of a paper was developed from this reed.
2. The metal the Hyksos used to make their weapons
4. Name by which the Pharaoh Khufu is sometimes known
5. The written language of ancient Egypt
6. The triangle area at the mouth of the Nile just before it empties into the ocean
7. Egypt's first capital
9. The part of ancient Egypt located to the south was called the _____ kingdom.

Name: _____   Date: _____

Egyptian Civilization Matching

Match the definition from the column on the right with the corresponding term in the column on the left. Place the letter of the definition on the blank next to the correct term.

_____ 1. Aten

_____ 2. Black Land

_____ 3. Canal

_____ 4. Chariots

_____ 5. Civil

_____ 6. Civilization

_____ 7. Dynasty

_____ 8. Hyksos

_____ 9. Khufu

_____ 10. Kingdoms

_____ 11. Linen

_____ 12. Lower

_____ 13. Mountains

_____ 14. Nile

_____ 15. Nubia

_____ 16. Pyramid

_____ 17. Red Land

_____ 18. Red Sea

_____ 19. Scribes

_____ 20. Thebes

A. The history of ancient Egypt is divided into three _____.

B. The part of ancient Egypt located in the northern delta where the river spreads out and empties into the Mediterranean Sea was called _____ Egypt.

C. The large river along which the Egyptian Civilization developed

D. The sea to the east of the Nile River

E. A series of rulers from the same family or line

F. An Egyptian tomb with a rectangular base and four triangular faces that meet at the top

G. The pharaoh buried in the Great Pyramid of Giza

H. People who kept records and wrote messages

I. King Mentuhotep made this city the capital during the Middle Kingdom

J. The country south of Egypt from which Egyptians brought gold, ivory, and slaves

K. Egypt was conquered by these people from Canaan. Their victory over the Egyptians marked the end of the Middle Kingdom.

L. The name of the sun god Pharaoh Amenhotep IV forced his people to worship

M. The culture developed by a particular region or nation

N. A war between two or more groups in the same country

O. Horse-drawn vehicles used in war

P. The Egyptians called their country the _____ _____ because of the fertile soil.

Q. The Egyptians called the desert surrounding their country the _____ _____.

R. The Nile River is fed by rain and melting snow from the _____ of northeastern Africa.

S. Rich Egyptians were wrapped in this material when they died.

T. The Egyptians built one of these between the Nile and the Red Sea in order to improve trade.

The Far East: China

Along with Mesopotamia, ancient Egypt, and the Indus Valley, ancient China was one of the world's earliest civilizations. Not very much is known about the beginnings of the Chinese Civilization. We do know, however, that like the other early civilizations, the Chinese Civilization developed on the banks of major rivers. As you have learned before, the fertile land beside rivers provided rich soil for farming and hunting, and water for drinking, irrigating crops, and fishing. The civilization of ancient China developed along the Huang He (Hwang Ho), or Yellow River. The Huang He is the second longest river in China. It flows east from the Tibetan highlands to the Yellow Sea in north China, with a length of about 3,000 miles. Villages also were developed along the Chang Jiang (Yangtze), the longest river in China.

The Huang He or Hwang Ho is sometimes called the Yellow River because of the color of the yellow mud it carries. Like the Nile, each year the Huang He overflows it banks, and when the flood water recedes, fertile mud is left behind. Crops grow well in this fertile soil, so it is not surprising that by around 5000 B.C., agricultural villages began to spring up along this river.

The Chinese Civilization began about 8000 years ago and still exists today. It is a rich culture that has contributed many things to the world. Since China's history is so long, space does not permit us to consider anything but the beginning of this intriguing civilization. The Xia (Hsia) Dynasty is considered to be the first dynasty of kings to rule China. The Hsia Dynasty lasted from around 2205 B.C. to 1766 B.C. During this period, the Chinese Civilization developed in a manner similar to the civilizations in the Near East. The Chinese built irrigation canals to water their crops, they made bronze, harvested silk, used the potter's wheel, and the soldiers used chariots.

The Xia dynasty was eventually replaced with the Shang Dynasty. The Shang Dynasty lasted from about 1766 B.C. to 1122 B.C. During this period, cities were carefully planned, and the people were divided into social ranks that ranged from royalty and nobles to slaves. While most people during this dynasty were farmers, craftsmen became more popular. Bronze-casting was developed at about this time.

During the ten major dynasties that followed the Shang Dynasty, trade flourished. Trade routes between Asia and the West were established, and silk became the main export of China. Silk is a very thin cloth made from cocoons spun by silkworms. Since silk was one of the most valuable items exported along the trade routes to West Asia and Europe, these routes became known as the Silk Roads. Other countries wanted to make silk for themselves, but the Chinese kept their methods of producing this cloth a secret until the fourth century A.D.

In ancient China, there were many gods, such as the earth god, the rain god, and the river god, but there was one god that was revered above all others. This was Shang Ti, "the Ruler Above."

The Chinese made sacrifices to the gods to ensure good crops, success in battle, and good fortune. While the poor could only present food and wine to the gods in their temples, the rich sacrificed animals. On special occasions, such as the death of a king, humans were sacrificed. The humans who were sacrificed were often prisoners of war or slaves.

> ### CHINESE CIVILIZATION AT A GLANCE
>
> **WHERE:** Valleys of the Huang He and Chang Jiang Rivers in Asia
>
> **WHEN:** Beginning about 5000 B.C.
>
> **ACHIEVEMENTS:**
> - Discovered and cultivated silk
> - Built the Great Wall of China
> - Invented gunpowder, rockets, magnetic compass, book printing, paper money, porcelain, and many more
> - Two great teachers lived in China—Confucius and Lao-tzu

The ancient Chinese believed that when a person died, he or she went to live with Shang Ti and that one's dead ancestors could influence life on Earth for his or her family. They believed their ancestors had powers to help them make wise decisions or to punish them. Therefore, the Chinese worshipped their ancestors. To please their ancestors, the Chinese built temples. They held many celebrations to honor their ancestors.

Perhaps as great as the technological contributions the Chinese made to the world were the philosophical contributions made by two great teachers who lived in China. One was Confucius, who lived from 551 B.C. to 479 B.C. Among other things, Confucius taught politeness, sincerity, unselfishness, respect for laws, and hard work. His beliefs have been written down, and his philosophy has become a religion called **Confucianism**.

Another philosopher who lived about the same time as Confucius was Lao-tzu. His beliefs were quite different from Confucius. Confucius thought people should improve society, but Lao-tzu taught that people should withdraw from society. He believed that people should live very simple lives in harmony with nature. He thought people should not try to be famous or rich but to be happy with what they had. He also thought people should sit quietly and meditate. His philosophy is called **Taoism** and comes from the word "tao," which means "way."

One of the great achievements of the ancient Chinese Civilization was the construction of the Great Wall of China, built to keep out invaders. Actually, the wall is not a single wall, but two stone walls that average about ten feet apart and run parallel to each other. The area between the walls is filled with earth and lined with stone, forming a road. The wall, which ran along the border between China and the territories in the north, is about 30 feet high and 1,500 miles long.

Construction of the Great Wall was not a single job. Many separate walls were built over 2,000 years. The wall began as an earthen wall supported by planks. It was built in segments by different states and each was only a few miles long. In about 221 B.C, Shi Huang Ti, the first Emperor of China, had these walls linked into one long wall. After the Qin Dynasty, other dynasties expanded and enlarged the wall until it was finished about 204 B.C. Even after the wall was completed, the Chinese continued working on it, making it more elaborate and modern in design. The stone wall, as we know it today, began during the Ming Dynasty, which lasted from A.D. 1368 to 1644. The remaining sections of the wall we see in photographs were built during this time. The wall built during the Ming Dynasty was strong, over 4,500 miles long, and was patrolled by 100,000 soldiers. Unfortunately, the entire length of the wall does not exist today. Parts of the wall have been taken down and used to build other structures.

The Chinese invented many things. Some of their inventions are the magnetic compass, crossbow, matches, moveable type, paper money, acupuncture, propeller, gunpowder, porcelain, umbrella, paper, wheelbarrow, seismograph, kite, cast iron, abacus, horse collar, rocket, brandy, whiskey, the game of chess, lacquer, and many others.

The Great Wall of China

Name: _____   Date: _____

Chinese Inventions and Discoveries
Crossword Puzzle Clues

Complete the crossword puzzle on page 24 using the clues below about Chinese inventions and discoveries.

ACROSS

3. Without this invention, humans would never have gotten to the moon.
5. Ben Franklin got a charge out of using this invention.
6. The moldboard ____ made of cast iron had a central ridge ending in a sharp point that cut the soil, and wings that pushed the soil off. It was said to have begun the agricultural revolution when it came to Holland.
9. A mechanical bow and arrow
11. Hard and brittle, ____ iron is formed into a particular shape by pouring the liquid metal into a mold.
12. The discovery of the ____ of the blood is generally credited to William Harvey in 1628. However, it was discussed in a medical manual in the second century B.C. in China.
15. Used to propel bullets from guns
17. The medical practice of sticking pins in the body to relieve pain or cure illnesses
18. A liquid used in printing
20. It's hard to believe that little worms can produce this beautiful thread.
21. Without ____ type, printing books would have been difficult.
23. A hard, white, translucent ceramic material used to make china
24. Without this twisted blade, some planes could not fly and ships could not move.

DOWN

1. Using a ____ to start a fire is better than rubbing two sticks together.
2. Used to protect one from the rain or sun
4. A board game for two players that is similar to medieval warfare
7. A glossy, clear finish applied to many kinds of materials
8. We couldn't celebrate Independence Day without them.
10. An instrument that measures earthquakes
11. A device that helps travelers go in the right direction
13. Some call it a manual calculator.
14. Made of cellulose pulp, it is used for writing, drawing, and printing.
16. A one-wheeled vehicle with handles used to carry small loads
19. The horse ____ was a harness that enabled a single horse to haul a ton and a half.
22. Other civilizations used coins, but the Chinese pioneered the use of ____ money.

Name: _____   Date: _____

Chinese Inventions and Discoveries
Crossword Puzzle

Use the clues on page 23 to complete the puzzle below.

Name: _____ Date: _____

Reproduce a Chinese Invention

The Chinese invented many things. Here are some Chinese inventions you can make.

MAKE A KITE

Kites were more than toys. They were very important tools in ancient China. Kites were used in construction. Materials were lifted with a kite. Kites were used in battles as well. Messages attached to kites were flown over enemy lines until they reached their allies, and then the lines were cut, and the kites and the messages fell to the soldiers below. Kites with hooks and bait were used for fishing. Kites were even fitted with whistles to make musical sounds while flying.

Listed below are simple directions for making a kite. While a kite made in this way may fly, it will not be very durable. The purpose is to make a very colorful kite that might be similar to one made by the ancient Chinese. Directions for more durable and more sophisticated kites can be found in craft books.

Materials:
- Large sheet of construction paper
- String
- Paint
- Tissue or crepe paper

Directions:
- Fold the construction paper in half.
- Cut out the shape of your kite. You might choose the shape of a butterfly, bird, or dragon.
- Color your kite with watercolors or finger paint.
- When dry, tie the string to one end and attach tissue paper scraps to make a tail.

MAKE A BALLOON ROCKET

The Chinese originally used gunpowder for fireworks, but then they developed rockets that could be used in war. The materials needed are common household items.

Materials:
- Balloon
- String
- Paper clip
- Tape
- Straw

Directions:
- Inflate the balloon and close the end with a paper clip.
- Carefully tape the straw to the side of the balloon.
- Thread the string through the straw, stretch the string straight, and then tie the ends of the string to two different chairs that are placed apart.
- Release the paper clip.
- Since the air inside the balloon pushes out in all directions, when the paper clip is removed the air escapes out the open end. As the air escapes in one direction, it will push the balloon in the opposite direction along the string.

Name: _____ Date: _____

MAKE A COMPASS

The magnetic needle compass made sea navigation possible. While this invention revolutionized history, you can make one in a few minutes with materials you have around your house.

Materials:
- Needle
- Magnet
- Cup of water
- Tape
- Slice of cork
- Marking pen

Directions:
- Magnetize the needle by stroking one end of a magnet along the entire length of it about 20 or 30 times. Always stroke in the same direction.
- Tape the needle to a broad, flat cork, and float the cork in the cup of water. The needle will rotate until it's pointing in a North-South direction. Since you probably know which general direction is north, use the magic marker, to place a spot on the end of the needle that points to the north.

MAKE MOVEABLE TYPE

The Chinese invented printing with moveable type, which made it possible to publish books faster and cheaper. This was four hundred years before Gutenberg printed the Bible. Because of the complexity of Chinese writing, however, it was not widely used.

Materials needed to make a printing block:
- Sharp kitchen knife which should be used only under the supervision of the teacher
- One small, unpeeled potato
- Marking pen
- Paper
- Water
- Small sponge
- Tempera or acrylic paint
- Newspaper

Directions:
- The student or teacher should cut the potato in half.
- With the marker, draw your initials on the part of the potato you have just cut. Since the stamp will print backwards, make sure you draw your initials backwards.
- Either the student or teacher should cut away the potato around the initials you drew. Make sure the initials stick up about 1/4 inch.
- Dampen the sponge and then dip it in paint.
- Place the sponge on the newspaper, press your stamp against the sponge, and then press the stamp against your paper. Your initials should be printed. It may be necessary to recarve part of your initials if they are not quite right.

The Mongols

If historians judged a civilization or culture by how long they existed, the Mongols would hardly be considered. Their empire lasted only a fraction as long as the Egyptian or the Roman Civilizations. Yet, in the span of 185 years, the Mongol Empire became the largest, most powerful, and most feared empire the world has ever known.

Just north of the Gobi Desert, between Siberia and northwest China, is a large area called the steppes. The word *steppe* is a Slavic word that means "grasslands." It is similar to the prairie in North America or the pampas in South America. The steppe is a harsh land that is very hot in the summer and very cold in the winter. Temperatures range from 40 degrees below zero in the winter to over 100 degrees in the summer. In the 11th century A.D., the steppe was home to several nomadic tribes. One of these tribes was the Mongols. As nomadic people, they moved as the seasons changed in order to have grass for grazing their sheep and horses. In winter they moved their sheep and horses to the south, to find new grazing lands and to get away from the cold. In the summer, they moved north again to find pasture for their flocks and herds and also to get away from the heat.

For many centuries, the Mongols were a number of independent tribes that often fought with one another. All of the Mongol tribes were made up of excellent horsemen, and some included hunters. It was said that the Mongols were so fast they could outrun animals. With their horses, they chased deer and antelope and were able to either kill them with arrows or lasso them. All of these qualities made the Mongols outstanding warriors.

The Chinese had always been afraid of the Mongol warriors who lived close to their borders. The Chinese built a great wall to keep them out, but the Mongols often scaled the wall and attacked them anyway. Early in the 13th century, China's greatest fear came to pass. The independent Mongolian tribes that they feared were united by Genghis Khan into a powerful nation eager to expand its empire.

When Genghis Khan was born, his name was Temujin, but he gave himself the title "Genghis Khan" when he became chief of his tribe. Genghis Khan means "mighty lord." Genghis Khan was an excellent general and one of the greatest conquerors of all time. He was disciplined, was well organized, and planned his strategy carefully. Genghis Khan's ability, coupled with the use of modern weapons, enabled the Mongol armies to be victorious in spite of the fact they were outnumbered in most of their battles.

In 1211, Genghis Khan led the Mongols in an invasion of the Chin Empire in northern China. This first raid led to many others, and eventually the empire established by Genghis Khan and his successors covered an area that included the countries that today are known as China, Korea, Russia, India, much of the Middle East, and all the area in between.

The Mongols were known for their brutality. They routinely destroyed everything that stood in their path. Everyone was the enemy. They not only killed soldiers, but also women, children, and animals. They would sometimes conquer a town, kill everyone in it, and then burn it down. The Mongols were ruthless, but at the same time, they were smart.

After Genghis Khan died in 1227, the empire was divided among his four sons, and it continued to expand. The grandsons of Genghis Khan successfully conquered most of Asia and parts of Europe. The enormous size of the empire made it difficult to maintain and administer, though. Eventually, the conquered people became stronger and were able to drive the Mongols out of their lands.

Name: _____ Date: _____

Mongol Civilization Quiz

Shown below are a number of sentences. Some are true and some are false. If the sentence is true, write "true" in front of the sentence. If the sentence is false, write a term that could replace the word in bold type to make the sentence true.

_____ 1. Genghis Khan means "**excellent horseman**."

_____ 2. Mongols were **excellent** horsemen.

_____ 3. The **steppe** is very hot in the summer and very cold in the winter.

_____ 4. The grandsons of Genghis Khan conquered most of **Australia** and parts of Europe.

_____ 5. After Genghis Khan died in 1227, the Mongol Empire was divided among his four **wives**.

_____ 6. The Mongols were ruthless and **stupid**.

_____ 7. The Mongol Empire lasted **185** years.

_____ 8. Genghis Khan was an **incompetent** general.

_____ 9. **Mongols** not only killed soldiers, they would kill women, children, and even animals.

_____ 10. In the 11th century, the steppe was home to several **nomadic** tribes.

_____ 11. The **Gauls** had always been afraid of Mongols who lived close to their borders.

_____ 12. The Mongol Empire included China, Korea, Russia, India and most of the Middle **East**.

_____ 13. The **Hittite** Empire was the largest and most feared empire the world has ever known.

_____ 14. The **Egyptians** built a great wall to keep the Mongols out of China.

Name: _____ Date: _____

Mongol Civilization Quiz (continued)

_____ 15. **Genghis Khan** was disciplined, well organized, and planned his strategy carefully.

_____ 16. When Genghis Khan was born, his name was **Steve**.

_____ 17. **Genghis Khan** was one of the greatest conquerors of all time.

_____ 18. North of the Gobi Desert, between Siberia and northwest China, are the **pampas**.

_____ 19. The independent **Indian** tribes were united by Genghis Khan.

_____ 20. After Genghis Khan died, the Mongol empire continued to **decrease**.

_____ 21. Legend has it that the Mongols were so **fast** they could outrun animals.

_____ 22. The word "steppe" is a Slavic word that means **desert**.

_____ 23. With their **horses**, Mongols chased and caught or killed deer and antelope.

_____ 24. For many centuries, the Mongols were a just a number of **independent** tribes.

_____ 25. Temperatures on the **steppes** range from 40 degrees below zero to over 100 degrees.

_____ 26. In 1211, Genghis Khan led the Mongols in an invasion of the Chin Empire in **Turkey**.

_____ 27. The steppe is similar to the **forests** in North America.

_____ 28. The Mongols were **outnumbered** in most of their battles.

_____ 29. The Mongols often conquered a town, **killed** everyone in it, and then burned it down.

_____ 30. As nomadic people, Mongols moved as the **neighbors** changed.

_____ 31. The steppe is similar to the **Andes** in South America.

_____ 32. The enormous **size** of the Mongol empire made it difficult to maintain and administer.

_____ 33. The Mongols were known for their **gentleness**.

_____ 34. Some Mongols were **hunters**.

_____ 35. Before they were united, the Mongol tribes often **fought** with each other.

The Indus Valley

The fertility of the Indus Valley, located in the western part of South Asia, lured farmers to its banks in about 2500 B.C. The people who lived along the Indus River developed one of the world's first great urban civilizations. Archaeologists call this civilization the Harappan Culture or Indus Civilization. This civilization originated in what is today Pakistan and western India and developed at about the same time as the early city-states of Egypt and Mesopotamia. Like Egypt and Mesopotamia, the civilization was established and grew as a result of its proximity to a river. The soil was also good for farming because the Indus River floods yearly, leaving behind fertile silt. Unlike the Egyptians and Mesopotamians, though, very little was known about this ancient civilization until recently. In 1921, an Indian archaeologist discovered remnants of a large city named Harappa.

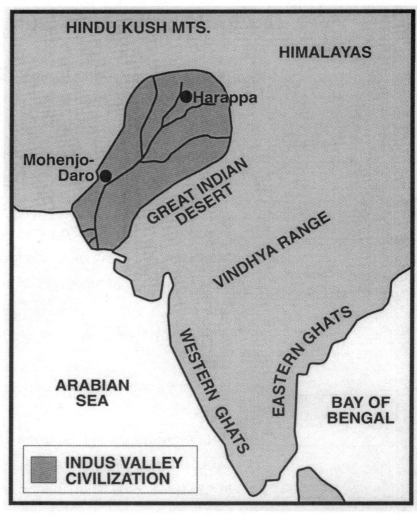

Harappa was one of the centers of the Indus Valley Civilization. The other, located about 350 miles away, was Mohenjo-daro. These two large cities were the homes of merchants and craftsmen. Harappa and Mohenjo-daro, along with other cities that have been excavated, indicate the people of this culture planned their cities carefully before they built them. The buildings were neatly arranged according to a grid system. They had long, perfectly straight streets and side alleys. Each city had a large granary and water tank as well as homes made of bricks and plaster. The houses were large with several rooms that led into a courtyard. Some of the homes had wells for drinking water and bathing, bathrooms with toilets, and a system for drainage. In fact, the builders of Mohenjo-daro designed and built one of the world's first drainage and sewage systems for a city. Pipes and drains carried water and waste away from the buildings to places outside the cities. There were openings along the streets that served the same purpose as modern manholes. Workers were able to climb down these openings into the drains and clear blockages.

The people of the Indus Civilization built a complex system of canals and dams for irrigation and flood management of the Indus River. They practiced communal farming. On these large farms, they grew barley, rice, wheat, dates, and cotton. They were one of the first civilizations known to have domesticated animals. They raised cattle, chickens, and buffalo. The farmers used wheeled carts drawn by oxen to take their grain to the cities where it was stored in large granaries.

Those who did not farm or hunt were either tradesmen or craftsmen. Trading with others was natural since people of the Indus Civilization could travel by water along the rivers or along the coastline to other cultures. They bought gold from southern India, turquoise from Iran, silver and copper from Afghanistan, and jade from India. With these goods, craftsmen were able to make pottery, jewelry, sculptures, spears, and knives.

About 1750 B.C. the civilization began to decline. The country was rocked by earthquakes and floods that destroyed the irrigation system suppling water to the crops. Many buildings were also destroyed. For some reason, the people seemed to have lost their will to rebuild. Invaders caused many to abandon the Indus Valley. Although nomads lived in this region for a while, hundreds of years would pass before new cities were built.

> **INDUS CIVILIZATION AT A GLANCE**
> **WHERE:** Western part of South Asia in what is now Pakistan and western India
> **WHEN:** 2500 B.C.–1750 B.C.
> **ACHIEVEMENTS:**
> - Built dams and canals for irrigation
> - Well-planned cities
> - One of the world's first drainage and sewer systems for a city
> - Among the first people to cultivate cotton
> - Among the first people to domesticate animals

While the Indus Civilization was not as wealthy and did not contribute as much as the Egyptians, Sumerians, or the Chinese, they were able to clear the jungle, build an elaborate irrigation system, design large cities, and develop a culture in a rather short period of time.

A Statue Artifact From the Indus Valley Civilization

31

Name: _____   Date: _____

Indus Valley Civilization Synonyms

Shown below are several words used in the explanation of the Indus Valley Civilization. Look at each word written in boldface type and then find the word at the right that has almost the same meaning. Circle the correct synonym, and then write a sentence using that synonym on the line below each group of words.

1. **proximity**   A. proxy   B. near   C. far

_____

2. **merchant**   A. cook   B. merchandise   C. trader

_____

3. **urban**   A. city   B. country   C. urchin

_____

4. **fertile**   A. rich   B. sterile   C. dry

_____

5. **remnants**   A. pottery   B. flawless   C. fragments

_____

6. **craftsman**   A. sly   B. artisan   C. deceitful

_____

7. **grid**   A. framework   B. opening   C. drain

_____

8. **irrigation**   A. irritation   B. plow   C. water system

_____

9. **granary**   A. grandmother   B. silo   C. temple

_____

10. **canal**   A. lake   B. drain   C. waterway

_____

11. **excavated**   A. dug   B. evacuate   C. maintain

_____

Name: _____ Date: _____

| 12. | **nomads** | A. wanderers | B. happy | C. bums |

| 13. | **elaborate** | A. colorful | B. simple | C. intricate |

| 14. | **abandon** | A. dessert | B. desert | C. keep |

| 15. | **domesticated** | A. tame | B. domicile | C. animal |

| 16. | **decline** | A. rise | B. sink | C. forget |

| 17. | **drainage** | A. removal | B. refuse | C. water |

| 18. | **invader** | A. sailor | B. attacker | C. horseman |

| 19. | **silt** | A. sediment | B. salt | C. grass |

| 20. | **tradesman** | A. potter | B. merchant | C. artisan |

| 21. | **communal** | A. public | B. individual | C. religious |

| 22. | **rebuild** | A. destroy | B. increase | C. restore |

| 23. | **jungle** | A. gym | B. rain forest | C. prairie |

| 24. | **blockages** | A. barriers | B. departure | C. opening |

| 25. | **courtyard** | A. hotel | B. fence | C. open space |

The Aegean Civilizations

The civilizations that developed around Greece and the islands in the Aegean Sea are often called the Aegean Civilizations. While there is evidence that humans lived in Greece over 8,000 years ago, it wasn't until 3000 B.C. that the earliest signs of civilization actually began. Greek civilization can be divided into three distinct periods.

1. The **Early Period** is sometimes called the Bronze Age. This period lasted from 3000 B.C. to 1150 B.C. Many of the legends written by Homer were stories that supposedly happened in this period.
   - The **Minoan** culture thrived on the island of Crete from sometime before 2000 B.C. to 1450 B.C.
   - The **Mycenaean** culture developed on the Greek mainland and reached its height about 1600 B.C. It lasted for about 400 years.
2. The **Middle Period** is sometimes called the "Dark Ages." It lasted from about 1100 B.C. until about 800 B.C. During the Middle Period, the culture declined. The people living in what we call Greece organized themselves not into one great nation, but rather into several city-states. Each city-state was a separate unit that governed itself.
3. The **Classical Period** began about 800 B.C. and lasted until 323 B.C. This is the period that includes the Golden Age of Greece when democracy, drama, philosophy, science, literature, and other accomplishments of this great culture reached their peaks. The city-states of Athens and Sparta, which represented two very different ideals, thrived during the Classical Period. The period ended with the death of Alexander the Great, who had conquered Persia and spread the Greek culture from Egypt to India. Eventually, the Romans conquered all of the land that had belonged to Greece.

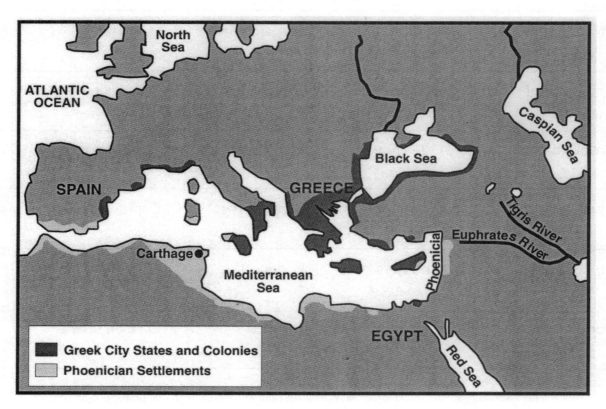

The Early Period: The Minoans

Named after their king Minos, the Minoan Civilization was the first civilization in Europe. The Minoan culture thrived on the island of Crete and other islands in the Aegean from sometime before 2000 B.C. to 1450 B.C. Crete is a large island between Asia Minor and Greece. Since Crete is an island and is relatively isolated from the rest of the world, the Minoan Civilization was not as concerned with invasion as those civilizations on the continent. While civilizations on the continent had to spend much of their time and resources developing armies and weapons, those living on Crete were free to concentrate on economic growth. This made it possible for the Minoans to grow enough food so that not everyone had to farm or hunt. Some were free to create art, fashion jewelry, or to make items that people used. Still others became merchants trading food and items with those living on other Aegean islands and those living on the continent. Minoans exported oil, wine, jewelry, and crafts. They imported many raw materials.

The wealth produced by trade had two effects, which were very unusual in the ancient world. The first was **social equality**. In most ancient civilizations, there were distinct classes. There was the nobility, which included rulers and priests. Members of this class were often wealthy and had a relatively easy life. Most of the others were poor and led a very difficult existence. On Crete, while some were wealthier than others, most people prospered enough to have enough food and live in fairly large homes. Even women seemed to be treated well, which was rare in the ancient world.

The second benefit of the wealth created by trading was that the Minoans became one of the first societies in history in which humans had enough **leisure time** to devote to activities not directly related to survival. Prior to this time, humans spent most of their waking hours finding, gathering, hunting, or growing food, finding or building shelter, making weapons, or protecting themselves from others. Free from these worries, many Minoans became interested in other activities such as sports. The two most popular sports on Crete were boxing and bull-jumping.

Bull-jumping is not the same as bullfighting, which most people today are familiar with. In fact bull-jumping is more dangerous and requires more courage, skill, and strength than bullfighting. Here's how it was done. A bull was released, and it would run at a jumper or at several jumpers. When the bull was close enough, the jumper would take the bull by the horns and either jump onto the bull's back or leap over the bull, turn a somersault in the air, and then land on his feet behind or beside the bull. While this maneuver is difficult and dangerous enough, it became even more difficult and dangerous when a jumper would grab a charging bull's horns and the bull would violently jerk its head up, propelling the jumper further into the air. The bull-jumper had to adjust to this momentum and land gracefully. Both young men and young women, dressed in male clothes, participated in this sport.

The great wealth created by trade also enabled Minoans to spend a great deal on building. Minoans built many towns and each one was centered on a palace. The palaces were quite large. One palace at Knossos covered over three acres and had over 1,000 rooms. Its

---

MINOAN CIVILIZATION AT A GLANCE

WHERE: Crete, a large island between Asia Minor and Greece

WHEN: 2000 B.C.–1450 B.C.

ACHIEVEMENTS:

- The first civilization in Europe
- One of the first social cultures with social equality
- Built elaborate palaces and large homes for its citizens
- Women were treated more fairly than in other cultures of the time
- Unlike other cultures, sports were enjoyed as a recreational activity, not just a religious ritual

---

walls were painted with scenes showing sporting events and other everyday activities in Knossos. Some of the Minoan palaces even had simple plumbing systems with toilets.

Minoans also built large comfortable homes for all the people, including the poor. The homes of the ordinary people consisted of many rooms and were often two stories high. On the first floor was a storeroom and upstairs were the living quarters. They had terraces and lightwells. Archaeologists have discovered that some homes were even five stories high. Contrast this with the single-roomed house that was common in the rest of the world for many centuries after the Minoans.

The Minoans lived a peaceful, prosperous existence on Crete for about five centuries. Then in 1450 B.C. they were conquered by the Mycenaeans who had developed a civilization on the Greek mainland. Why were the Minoans conquered? No one is quite sure. Some say an earthquake, which caused widespread devastation to Crete, damaged their economy. Others suggest that the explosion of a volcano on a nearby island was so severe the volcanic ash ruined agriculture and the resulting tsunami leveled cities and destroyed harbors. Still others believe the fall of the Minoans was caused by invaders. No matter what the cause, a new power dominated the region in 1450 B.C. It was the Mycenaeans.

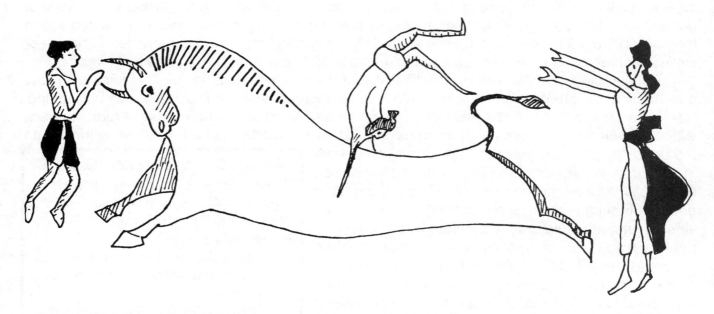

Young Minoan men and women participated in bull-jumping, a very dangerous sport. This sport, as well as boxing, were favorite leisure-time activities of the Minoans.

Name: _____ Date: _____

Minoan Civilization Quiz

Shown below are a number of sentences. Some are true and some are false. If the sentence is true, write "true" in front of the sentence. If the sentence is false, write a term that could replace the word in bold type to make the sentence true.

_____ 1. Not everyone had to farm or **hunt** in Minoa.

_____ 2. Minoans were free to devote most of their time and resources to **physical** growth.

_____ 3. A **stadium** at Knossos covered three acres and had 1,000 rooms.

_____ 4. Minoans **imported** oil, wine, jewelry, and crafts.

_____ 5. The Minoan civilization was named after king **Minos**.

_____ 6. The Minoan culture thrived on the island of **Sicily**.

_____ 7. The Minoan civilization was the first civilization in **Asia**.

_____ 8. The first civilization with **economic** equality was Minoa.

_____ 9. Most Minoans had enough food and lived in fairly **small** homes.

_____ 10. Minoans built many towns, each centered on a **palace**.

_____ 11. Minoan homes of **ordinary** people were often two stories high.

_____ 12. The two popular sports on Crete were boxing and **bull-throwing**.

_____ 13. Minoans built large comfortable homes for the **poor**.

_____ 14. The Minoan culture was one of the first societies in which humans had enough **leisure** time to devote to activities not directly related to survival.

_____ 15. Minoan women seemed to be treated **poorly**, which was not common in the ancient world.

_____ 16. Minoans traded with those living on other **Aegean** Islands as well as those living on the continent.

_____ 17. Crete is a large **peninsula** between Asia Minor and Greece.

_____ 18. In 1450 B.C. the Minoans were conquered by the **Romans**.

_____ 19. The Minoans lived peacefully for about **nine** centuries.

_____ 20. Both young men and young **women** were bull-jumpers.

The Early Period: The Mycenaeans

The Mycenaeans arrived in Greece about 2000 B.C. and lived on the mainland of Greece. Their civilization actually began around 1650 B.C., but they did not become dominant in the area until about 1450 B.C. Their supremacy lasted only approximately 200 years. In about 1200 B.C., they were attacked and their palaces were destroyed. We do not know who conquered the Mycenaeans.

The people of this culture are called Mycenaeans because the best-known city in their civilization was Mycenae. The Mycenaeans traded heavily with the Minoans on Crete and were strongly influenced by their culture. In 1450 B.C. when the Mycenaeans conquered the Minoans, they adopted much of the Minoan culture. One major difference between the Minoans and the Mycenaeans was their architecture. While the Minoan cities and palaces were unfortified, Mycenaean cities were heavily fortified and protected by huge stone walls. Invaders were common in Greece, and there were many wars. Living on the continent rather than on a relatively isolated island exposed the Mycenaeans to invasions.

Mycenaeans became rich by trading. The excess food they produced was traded on various islands and in cities on the mainland around the Mediterranean. In return, the Mycenaeans imported copper, tin, gold, and other items. They were so ambitious that they traded as far away as Mesopotamia and Western Europe. There is even evidence their trade may have extended as far away as Scandinavia and Russia. In addition to traders, they were warriors and mercenaries.

Most people probably haven't heard of the Mycenaeans, but they have probably heard of the *Iliad* and the *Odyssey*. The *Iliad* and the *Odyssey* are long poems called **epic poems** written by Homer, the blind Greek poet who lived in 800 B.C. These poems are about Mycenaean heroes. They were stories that had been told from generation to generation. The Greeks believed these stories were of actual occurrences from several centuries before. They were never written down before Homer because there was no alphabet before the Greeks learned the Phoenician alphabet. While there may have been a kernel of truth in the stories, it is likely that each generation changed and embellished the stories to make them more interesting and the characters more heroic.

The *Iliad* tells of King Agamemnon of Mycenae and how he and a group of Greek heroes went to war with Troy, a city on the coast of what is now Turkey. Legend says the war was fought over the kidnapping of Helen, the beautiful queen and wife of Menelaus, the brother of Agamemnon and King of Sparta. Historians believe the war was probably fought over land.

The war between the Greeks and Troy lasted for ten years because the strong wall that surrounded the city prevented Agamemnon and his men from entering Troy. The Greeks tricked the Trojans by building a large wooden horse, leaving it in front of the gate, and then sailing away. The Trojans brought the horse inside the city, and that night when everyone slept, Greek soldiers, who were hidden in the horse, opened the gates to the city. The Greek army, which had returned during the night, entered Troy and defeated the Trojans.

The *Odyssey* is the story of Odysseus and his long journey home after the Trojan war. During his journey, which lasts ten years, he has many adventures that involve gods, goddesses, and mortals.

MYCENAEAN CIVILIZATION AT A GLANCE

WHERE: On the mainland of Greece

WHEN: 1650 B.C.–1200 B.C.

ACHIEVEMENTS:

- Their leaders, warriors, and wars serve as the basis for much of Homer's *Illiad* and *Odyssey*
- The first Greek-speaking people
- Excellent traders and craftsmen

Name: _____   Date: _____

Greek Word Roots

Many of the words we use every day were taken from the Greeks. Below is a sample of some of the words that had their origins in ancient Greece. To the left is the definition of the word. You are to fill in the blanks at the right to complete the word that goes with the definition.

DEFINITION	TERM
1. Another name for a play	__ R __ M __
2. A long and adventurous trip	O D Y __ __ E Y
3. An institution designed for learning	__ __ __ O O __
4. Plain and simple	S P __ __ __ __ N
5. A room for indoor sports	__ Y __ __ __ S I U __
6. Keeps a boat in place	__ __ C H __ __ __
7. A funny play	C __ __ __ __ __
8. A play in which the main character suffers	T __ __ G __ __ __
9. A person who writes poetry	__ __ __ T
10. The study of numbers	__ __ T H __ __ __ T __ __ __
11. A system of values	P H __ __ __ S __ __ __ __
12. Another name for a dictator	__ Y R __ __ T
13. A person who rules	__ O N A __ __ __ H
14. The study of living things	__ __ __ __ __ __ G Y
15. A group of musicians playing together	__ R __ __ __ __ T R __
16. A name for an actor or actress	T __ __ S P __ __ N
17. The study of the effect of civilization on the environment	E __ __ __ __ __ __ Y
18. A brave person	__ __ __ O
19. The science of managing government	__ __ L __ __ I C S
20. Mathematics dealing with lines, angles, and solids	G __ O __ __ T R __
21. A course dealing with the rules of language	__ __ __ M M __ R
22. Government where all citizens help make decisions	D __ __ __ C R __ __ __
23. A cruel or mean leader	D __ C T __ __ __ R
24. This prevents the growth of germs	A N T __ __ __ P __ __ C
25. A building where people worship	__ __ U R __ __
26. One of a number of related events	E P __ S O __ __

The Middle Period: Athens and Sparta

After the fall of Mycenaea, Greece entered the Middle Period, which is sometimes called the Dark Ages. It lasted from about 1100 B.C. until about 800 B.C. During the Middle Period, the culture declined. Little is known about this period in Greek history since there are no written records. We do know there were various groups of people living in villages on the mainland as well as the islands in the Aegean Sea. Since these villages were separated by mountains and the sea, there was little contact among the various villages. As a result, each village was concerned with its own needs, not caring at all about those living in other villages. Gradually, the people organized themselves into several small city-states, almost like separate nations, each called a **polis**. Each polis was a separate unit that developed its own government. It not only consisted of the city, but included the area surrounding the city as well. Each polis had a marketplace called an **agora**. An area that was higher than the rest of the polis was called an **acropolis**. A wall to protect the polis was often built.

We consider all of the city-states in Greece to be the Greek Civilization, because they shared the same language, religion, and culture. However, the Greeks living in this time were not loyal to Greece as a nation, but to the city-state in which they lived. Many city-states began to develop during the Middle Period, but the best-known and most powerful were Athens and Sparta. People from Athens were called Athenians. Those living in Sparta were Spartans. Both were on the Peloponnesian Peninsula of Greece.

Athens and Sparta were just developing during the Middle Period, and they could not have been more different. One difference between the two was the manner in which they governed themselves. In order to understand how different Athens and Sparta were, it is important to understand how government developed in the Greek city-states. Several different types of government were tried over the years by the Greeks. At one time they had leaders similar to a king, but the people thought they could govern better than one person. So they established an aristocracy. An **aristocracy** is a government by a ruling class. The ruling class in this case was the land owners. This type of government was eventually replaced by an oligarchy. An **oligarchy** is run by only a few people. In the case of the Greeks, the rulers were the wealthiest in town. Many city-states eventually abandoned this type of government and established a democracy. A **democracy** is a government run by the people who are being governed. *Demos* is a Greek word that means "people." In the Greek democracy, all citizens were able to vote and to decide how the city-state was to be run. Slaves and women were not allowed to vote or participate.

Athens had a democracy. Every Athenian man, rich or poor, was a member of an assembly, which met to discuss issues concerning Athens. Each citizen was allowed to speak and give his opinion at these assemblies. Each year a council consisting of 500 citizens was chosen by lot. The council managed the city and decided what should be discussed at the assemblies. Citizens also took turns as judges and public officials. This open-minded attitude extended into other aspects of Athenian life. Artists, writers, philosophers, architects, and scientists flourished in Athens.

Sparta, on the other hand, was ruled by two kings and a council. They did not have a democracy. This type of government worked well for Spartans who were not interested in the "finer things in life" that the Athenians pursued. Spartan life was simple. There was no art, music, poetry, or fine clothing. They cared little for ideas or new invention. Their whole existence was built around war and military discipline. Beginning at age seven, all men were trained as soldiers. They were given little food and were treated harshly to make them ready for the hardships of war. Even women were required to become strong and healthy so that they could have strong and healthy children. The Spartan army was strong and feared throughout the area.

The Classical Period: The Golden Age of Greece

The Classical Period of Greece began about 800 B.C. and lasted until 323 B.C. Although there were periodic wars among the city-states, life was pretty good. Food was in abundance, craftsmen and artists produced objects that could be traded, and the Greeks had enough wealth to devote time to the arts, education, architecture, philosophy, and science. This is the period in which Greek culture reached its peak. It is sometimes called the Golden Age of Greece.

Greeks valued the world's first democracy they had created. All citizens were members of the governing body called the **assembly**. A citizen was a free man over 21 who was born to Athenian parents. The assembly met every nine days to make decisions on laws, building, and other matters of interest. Each citizen was not only able to vote on the matters that came before the assembly, he also had a right to speak at the assembly in order to influence the votes of others.

The Greeks understood that it was education that sustained their culture and their good life. However, only young men from wealthy families received an education. When a boy was seven, he was sent to a school. His education was divided into three sections: letters, music, and athletics.

The first section of a boy's education, called the letters, is what we would call the basics today. Students learned to read, write, and do arithmetic. They wrote on tablets coated with wax using a stylus. They learned to do arithmetic on the abacus. The abacus was a device consisting of a frame holding parallel rods strung with moveable beads. As they grew older, the boys were required to memorize poetry and learn the skill of debating.

Since music was an important part of Greek festivals and celebrations, it was an important part of Greek education. Music education consisted of learning about music and learning to sing and play a musical instrument. Greeks played the flute and stringed instruments. Girls were also trained to play these instruments.

At age fourteen, boys began their athletic training. They practiced wrestling, jumping, running, and throwing a discus and javelin. These are the same athletic activities found in the Olympic Games. The purpose of the athletic training was to prepare boys to fight in the army. At age 18 boys were trained as soldiers for two years.

Children of poor parents and those of slaves were not involved in education. They began working early in their lives. Girls did not go to school either. Some parents taught them at home, or if they were wealthy enough, they hired tutors to teach their children to read and write. For the most part, a girl's education consisted of learning to run a home and developing domestic skills.

The Greeks valued religion. They had many gods who ruled every aspect of their lives. There was a god of war, a god of music, and so on. The king of the gods was Zeus. It was thought that Zeus

---

CLASSICAL GREEK CIVILIZATION AT A GLANCE

WHERE: On the mainland of Greece and surrounding islands. Their influence was expanded to colonies around the Mediterranean Sea.

WHEN: 800 B.C.–323 B.C.

ACHIEVEMENTS:

- Formed the world's first democracy
- Produced the first dramas and developed drama as art
- Built magnificent buildings
- Created beautiful statues
- Wrote literature, poetry, and drama that are so outstanding they are still studied today
- Took a scientific approach to the study of medicine
- Were the first to write histories
- Developed a method of classifying plants
- Developed rules for geometry and made other mathematical contributions

and all of the other gods lived on Mount Olympus in the northern part of Greece. The Greeks built magnificent temples in which to worship their gods and made beautiful statues to honor them. They thought their gods were similar to humans, having the same emotions and human qualities. The stories of their gods are called **myths** and are still studied in school.

Drama, another important part of Greek life, grew out of religion. Greek playwrights developed the art of drama and wrote both comedies and tragedies in the honor of the gods. These dramas were performed at religious festivals. The audience sat in outdoor theaters built into the side of the hills. The actors and the chorus acted out the play on a level surface called the orchestra. Several of these theaters still exist and can be seen today. Some famous Greek playwrights were Euripides, Sophocles, Aeschylus, and Aristophanes.

Like drama, athletic competitions or games also developed from Greek religion. Athletic contests were held at religious festivals and even at funerals of famous people. The philosophy of Greeks living at this time was that a person should have a healthy mind in a healthy body. Athletes were given as much respect as philosophers, artists, and priests. Champion athletes were treated as national heroes. The Olympic Games originated in Olympia, Greece, in 776 B.C.

The Greeks also valued science and medicine. Many scientific advances were made by Greeks before the Classical Period, but it was medicine that received an emphasis in this period. While the Greeks believed that sickness was a punishment of the gods, they did develop procedures for treating sick people with herbs, special diets, and exercise. They studied sick people and diseases and developed treatments based on their research. A famous Greek physician was Hippocrates, who is known as the "Father of Modern Medicine." Although he wrote 53 books on science and medicine, most remember him because of the Hippocratic Oath, which was named after him. It is an oath that deals with ethics in medicine. Modern doctors still take the Hippocratic Oath before they begin their practices.

Beauty and knowledge were valued among the Greeks. Magnificent temples, sculpture, painting, music, pottery, and dance flourished during the Classical Period of Greece. Knowledge was as important as beauty. Ideas and knowledge about our physical world, as well as the nature of humans, expanded greatly. Pythagoras developed a theory that the world is based on mathematical patterns. Heraclitus developed a theory dealing with atoms. Euclid wrote a book on geometry. There were many great philosophers during this period. Some of the more famous were Socrates, Aristotle, and Plato.

The city-states of Athens and Sparta, which represented two very different ideals, reached their peaks during this period. Both were strong militarily. While Athens had the best navy, Sparta had the best army. In an effort to protect itself from the Persians, the Athenians suggested the various city-states unite into a league. It was named the Delian League. The members of the league provided money for an even stronger navy that defeated the Persians in 486 B.C.

Athens had bigger ideas, however. They sent their navy to attack smaller city-states in order to expand their empire. In retaliation, Sparta, who was not a member of the Delian League, joined forces with many smaller city-states to form the Peloponnesian League. In 431 B.C., the Peloponnesian League declared war on the Delian League.

The Peloponnesian War lasted for 27 years. While each side had victories, it was costly to all involved. Eventually, Sparta received help from the Persians, and the Athenians were defeated. Sparta began ruling over all of the city-states. Democracy had ended. The Spartans were not good at ruling, and for 30 years there were many battles and wars. Greece became so weak that when the Spartans were attacked by a force from Thebes, the Spartans were defeated.

Name: _____ Date: _____

Athens and Sparta Quiz

Listed below are statements that relate to either Athens or Sparta. Before each statement are the letters "A" which represents Athens, and "S" which represents Sparta. Circle the letter to which the statement refers.

A S   1. They did not have a democracy.

A S   2. Citizens of this city took turns as judges and public officials.

A S   3. Were not interested in the "finer things in life"

A S   4. Each citizen of this city was permitted to speak at the assembly.

A S   5. Each year a council consisting of 500 citizens was chosen by lot.

A S   6. Had no art, music, poetry, or fine clothing

A S   7. Had a democracy

A S   8. Had a very simple life

A S   9. Had an open-minded attitude

A S   10. Cared little for ideas or new invention

A S   11. Every man, rich or poor, was a member of the assembly.

A S   12. Was ruled by two kings and a council

A S   13. Had the best navy

A S   14. Created art and fine buildings

A S   15. Was not a member of the Delian League

A S   16. Formed the Peloponnesian League

A S   17. Had the best army

A S   18. Beginning at age seven, all men were trained as soldiers.

A S   19. They were given little food and treated harshly to make them ready for the hardships of war.

A S   20. Formed the Delian League

A S   21. Philosophy thrived in this city.

A S   22. Women were required to become strong and healthy so that they could have strong and healthy children.

A S   23. Understood that an education sustained their culture and their good life

A S   24. Their whole existence was built around war and military discipline.

A S   25. Were defeated by a force from Thebes

A S   26. High-ranking governmental administrators and generals were elected.

A S   27. Scientists and architects lived in this city.

A S   28. Many great artists and thinkers lived here.

A S   29. Received help from the Persians and won the Peloponnesian War

A S   30. Had a council of 500 citizens who managed the city and decided what should be discussed at the assemblies

Name: _____ Date: _____

Become a Myth Maker

Prior to the ancient Greeks, there was little scientific understanding of the world and how it worked. Stories involving the Greek gods were created to explain things such as thunder, lightning, earthquakes, and other phenomenon. These kinds of stories are called **myths**. Myths involve heroes, gods, and supernatural beings and are used to explain customs, ways of life, or aspects of the world in which we live. A collection of myths is referred to as **mythology**. The Greeks had an extensive mythology that developed from their religion.

In ancient Greece, the people believed that the gods and goddesses lived in a beautiful palace so high on Mount Olympus it could not be seen by humans. The Greeks also believed their gods were immortal, which means they lived forever. According to Greek mythology, there was a god who ruled every aspect of life. Ares was the god of war, Apollo was the god of music, Athena was the goddess of learning, and so on. In addition, there were stories about each of the gods that told how they were born, who their parents were, and what activities they participated in.

ASSIGNMENT: CREATE AN ORIGINAL MYTH

In order to complete this assignment, you will need to read and study a number of Greek myths. You will find that some myths explain a natural phenomenon. Here is an example of a Greek myth that was developed to explain the phenomenon of echoes.

WHY THERE IS AN ECHO

Zeus, the king of the gods, was married to Hera. Hera was very suspicious of Zeus since he had been unfaithful in the past. On one occasion, Hera believed that Zeus was spending time with the wood nymphs and worried that Zeus might be falling in love with them. One day Hera decided to check up on Zeus, but Echo, who was also a nymph, prevented her from searching by engaging her in a long conversation. When Hera realized that Echo's purpose was to prevent her from finding Zeus and the wood nymphs together, she decreed that from that day forward, Echo's speech would be limited to repeating what others said. Echo eventually fell in love with Narcissus who rejected her. Her grief caused her to gradually fade away until only the sound of her voice remained.

Other myths deal with an emotion such as love, hate, envy, jealousy, or fear. Here is an example of a myth dealing with love and sadness.

ORPHEUS AND EURYDICE

Orpheus (pronounced or-fee-us) was the greatest musician on Earth. Only the gods could play and sing better. Orpheus and a young maiden named Eurydice (pronounced yoo-rid-i-see) fell in love and were married. However, just after the wedding, she was bitten by a viper, and she died. Orpheus was grief-stricken, and he decided to go down to the underworld and plead for his wife to be brought back to life. As he played and sang his request, Hades and the other inhabitants of the underworld were so touched that Hades decided to allow Eurydice to return to the world of the living, but only on one condition. Orpheus could not look at Eurydice until they were both out of the underworld. Orpheus went first, and he didn't look back until he was above ground in the sunshine. However, Eurydice had not yet stepped out of the shadows of the underworld, and as he reached for her, she disappeared back to the underworld. Orpheus was not permitted to enter the underworld again, so he wandered the countryside playing sadly until he too died.

Name: _____   Date: _____

CREATE AN ORIGINAL MYTH

After you have read a few other Greek myths and learned more about the Greek gods and goddesses, you are to write an original Greek myth using one of the Greek gods. Your myth can explain a natural phenomenon, teach a moral truth, or deal with an emotion. Here is a partial list of Greek gods.

CHIEF GREEK GODS AND GODDESSES

1. Zeus - king and father of the gods
2. Poseidon - god of the sea and earthquakes
3. Hera - queen of the gods and guardian of marriage
4. Athena - goddess of wisdom, war, patriotism, good citizenship, and protector of Athens
5. Apollo - god of poetry, music, medicine, and light
6. Artemis - goddess of hunting, wild things, and the moon
7. Ares - god of war
8. Hephaestus - god of fire, the blacksmith god
9. Aphrodite - goddess of love and beauty
10. Hermes - messenger of the gods; god of science and invention
11. Hestia - goddess of the hearth and home
12. Demeter - goddess of grain and agriculture

OTHER IMPORTANT GODS

13. Hades - god of the underworld
14. Eros - god of love (Cupid)
15. Pan - god of the woods and fields (half man and half goat)
16. Dionysus - god of wine, revelry, dancing, and drama

MINOR DIVINITIES

17. Nymphs (Dryads and Nereids) - guarded different parts of nature
18. Muses - goddesses of various arts, mostly literary
     Terpsichore - Muse of choral song and dance
     Euterpe - Muse of lyric poetry
     Erato - Muse of love poetry
     Polyhymnia - Muse of sacred poetry (hymns)
     Thalia - Muse of comic drama
     Calliope - Muse of epic poetry
     Melpomene - Muse of tragic drama
     Urania - Muse of astronomy
     Clio - Muse of history
19. Fates - goddesses who controlled the destiny of every mortal person
     Clotho - spun the bright threads of youth
     Lachesis - distributed the threads of life; directed the destinies of mortals
     Atropos - symbol of death, cut the threads of life

On a separate sheet of paper, answer the following questions and then write your myth.

1. What is the title of your myth?
2. Who are the gods or goddesses involved in your myth?
3. What is your myth about? (emotion, natural phenomenon, moral truth, etc.)

Name: _____ Date: _____

Make an Advertisement Using a Greek or Roman God

Greek and Roman gods are sometimes used in advertising. Pictures of Hermes, or his Roman counterpart Mercury, the Greek messenger of the gods, are used by florists to show they deliver fast. Poseidon, or Neptune, the ruler of the seas, is used to advertise seafood restaurants or cruises. Your assignment is to create an advertisement for a modern product using a Greek or Roman god or mythical creature. Choose a god or creature that has qualities you want your customer to associate with your product. Use the gods and goddesses from the list on the previous page, or you can find others with a little research. An example of an ad using the mythical creature Medusa, who had snakes for hair, is given below.

Hard-to-Tame Hair?

Lock your Locks

With

Clenched Satin

Even if your hair is as wild as Medusa's of Greek Mythology,
Clenched Satin can help.

More than just an ordinary hair spray,
Clenched Satin adds body and sheen and holds your hair in place all day long.

The Macedonians: Alexander the Great

For a time, the city-state of Sparta ruled Greece. The Spartan soldiers were known for their bravery and fighting skills, so it is very surprising that the Spartans were conquered by a smaller army from Thebes in 371 B.C. The Theban army was able to accomplish the remarkable feat by using a military maneuver. The soldiers arranged their formation into the shape of a crescent. When the Spartans attacked, the Theban army surrounded them.

Thebes only ruled for a few years, however. In 359 B.C., Philip II became king of Macedonia. **Macedonia**, or Macedon as it is sometimes called, was a large area north of Greece. It was a rugged, mountainous country, and the people living there were much different than the Greeks. The Greeks considered themselves very cultured and civilized, but they felt the Macedonians were barbarians.

Philip was destined to lead the Macedonians to defeat the Greek city-states and become the leader of Greece. Philip strengthened his army and eventually defeated all of the Greek city-states to form one large country. His goal was to combine the strength of all of the Greeks and defeat the Persians. But in 336 B.C., Philip was assassinated and his son, Alexander, became king.

As a young man, Alexander was raised with the sons of other important Macedonians and Greeks. They studied, played games, and learned about warfare. In addition to being a great warrior, Alexander was also a scholar. His tutor was Aristotle who trained him in rhetoric, philosophy, history, and literature and encouraged his interest in medicine and science.

In 336, when Alexander rose to power, the empire was in disorder. Alexander, as well as Macedonia, had many enemies. His first act was to order the execution of those who had killed his father. Then he began to restore order to his small empire. He suppressed a revolt in Thessaly, just south of Macedonia. His success in battle resulted in his being chosen to be general of the Greek forces. Alexander was only 20 years old at the time.

After uniting the old city-states of Greece, Alexander decided to attack Persia, Greece's old enemy, just as his father had planned. Alexander and his army were successful in his attack. The Persian leader, King Darius III, and his army were defeated. Alexander went on to expand his empire by invading Egypt, the Indus Valley, and eastern Iran.

Alexander was aware that since his empire was so large, it would be impossible for it to be ruled from a central location, so he established Greek colonies in countries he had just defeated. These colonies were run by Alexander's soldiers.

Alexander was returning from his conquests in India when he died of a fever in 323 B.C. He was only 32 years old. In only ten years, he had taken control of almost the entire known world. However, with Alexander dead, the empire began to crumble. Some of his generals killed Alexander's son so that he could not become ruler. The generals fought over the kingdom, and eventually it was divided into three kingdoms, each ruled by one general. One ruled Persia, another ruled Macedonia, and another ruled Egypt. The Greek language and culture remained a dominant part of these areas for several hundred years after the death of Alexander the Great.

ALEXANDER'S EMPIRE AT A GLANCE

WHERE: From Greece to India

WHEN: 359 B.C.–323 B.C.

ACHIEVEMENTS:
- Established the largest empire of the time, which included almost all of the known world
- Established large cities, including Alexandria, Egypt
- Spread Greek culture to a large part of the world

Name: _____ Date: _____

Map of Alexander the Great's Empire

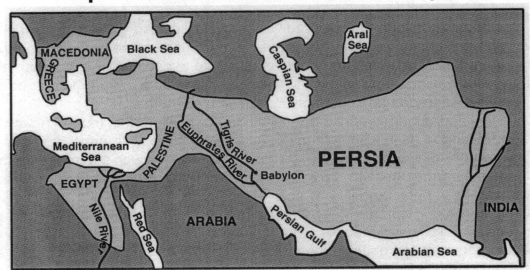

Alexander the Great Quiz

Shown below are a number of sentences. Some are true and some are false. If the sentence is true, write "true" in front of the sentence. If the sentence is false, write a term that could replace the word in bold type to make the sentence true.

_____ 1. After Alexander's death, his empire was divided into **three** parts.

_____ 2. Alexander was tutored by **Pluto.**

_____ 3. Sparta believed in a strong **navy**.

_____ 4. The Greeks thought the **Egyptians** were barbarians.

_____ 5. Greek **city-states** often fought among themselves.

_____ 6. Macedon was a large area North of **India**.

_____ 7. When Alexander became king, his first act was to order the execution of those who had killed his **father**.

_____ 8. Philip II was the ruler of **Persia**.

_____ 9. Alexander established Greek **colonies** to rule his empire.

_____ 10. Alexander died when he was **thirty-two** years old.

_____ 11. Darius III was king of **Macedonia**.

_____ 12. Alexander was a **scholar**.

_____ 13. Sparta was defeated by the **Persians**.

_____ 14. **Alexander** established the largest empire in the ancient world.

_____ 15. **Darius** died of a fever.

_____ 16. Philip was killed by **assassins**.

_____ 17. After Alexander died, his **wife** was murdered.

Ancient Europe: The Etruscans

The Etruscans were an ancient people who lived in what is now central Italy. Italy is a country shaped like a boot surrounded by the Mediterranean Sea. Etruria rose to prominence from about 800 B.C. until 300 B.C. It was the first great civilization on the Italian peninsula, and it greatly influenced the Romans who overthrew the Etruscan king about 500 B.C.

Where the Etruscan people came from is unclear. Some believe they came from Asia. Others feel they had always lived in Italy and their culture was developed by contact with Greeks and Carthaginians. It is apparent the Etruscans were influenced by the Greeks. The major Etruscan gods were similar to those of Greece. The Etruscan alphabet is based on the Greek alphabet. The Etruscans even decorated their tombs with scenes from Greek mythology. It is also apparent that the Etruscans passed much of their culture to the Romans.

While we are not sure where the Etruscans originally came from, there is no debate about where they lived. The Etruscans lived between the Tiber River in the south and the Arno River in the north. This is the area Italians call **Tuscany**. The Etruscan Culture stretched from Campania in the south to the Po Valley in the north.

Etruria was very wealthy because of its fertile land and rich mineral ore resources. Etruscans traded with the Greeks, Phoenicians, and with people as far away as France, Spain, and Africa. While they had exceptional harbors that promoted trade, most Etruscan cities were several miles inland from the ocean. This protected them from piracy.

The Etruscans were more advanced than the Romans in the seventh century B.C. They conquered Rome and ruled them for about 100 years. However, Etruria was not an empire as we generally think of empires. They had no strong central government. Instead there were a number of city-states. The Etruscans formed a league of 12 cities; each was ruled by a priest-king called a **lucomon**. The lucomon was elected each year and was selected from the nobility that governed each city.

The Etruscans were excellent engineers. Their cities were well planned with bridges, canals, and temples. They had paved streets and brick houses. Most cities were arranged in the form of a quadrangle, with two main streets that intersected. The cities were often surrounded by walls for protection. The streets were well drained and designed to bear heavy traffic. In order to drain the Forum in Rome, a drain and a pattern of underground water tunnels were built throughout the city.

Over time the Romans became increasingly powerful, and the Etruscan Civilization was absorbed by the Roman Republic. This happened by the third century B.C., and the Etruscan culture gradually disappeared, although their language did continue to be used for some religious ceremonies.

While Roman writers indicate they did not think highly of the Etruscans, they were greatly influenced by them. They were influenced by their art, architecture, and religion. The toga was originally an Etruscan ceremonial garment. Purple was considered the royal color by the Etruscans. Rome, and eventually many cultures, adopted this color to signify royalty. The Etruscans also gave the Romans the alphabet, writing, and many different crafts.

ETRUSCAN EMPIRE AT A GLANCE

WHERE: Central Italy in what is now called Tuscany

WHEN: 800 B.C.–300 B.C.

ACHIEVEMENTS:
- Cities were well planned with paved streets and brick houses
- Skilled craftsmen
- Women had more freedom than the women in Greece or Rome
- Excellent sailors
- Built drains and underground water tunnels to remove excess water

Name: _____   Date: _____

Etruscan Civilization Quiz

Shown below are a number of sentences. Some are true and some are false. If the sentence is true, write "true" in front of the sentence. If the sentence is false, write a term that could replace the word in bold type to make the sentence true.

_____ 1. In the seventh century B.C., the Etruscans were more **advanced** than the Romans.

_____ 2. The Etruscans conquered **Macedonia** and ruled them for about 100 years.

_____ 3. The Etruscan Civilization was eventually absorbed by the **Greek** Republic.

_____ 4. The Etruscans lived between the **Tigris** River in the south and the Arno river in the north.

_____ 5. Most Etruscan cities were arranged in the form of a **triangle**.

_____ 6. Each Etruscan city was ruled by a **priest-king**.

_____ 7. Italy is a country surrounded by the **Black** Sea.

_____ 8. Etruria was **destitute** because of fertile land and rich mineral ore.

_____ 9. The Etruscans were excellent **engineers**.

_____ 10. Etruria rose to prominence from about 800 B.C. until **300** B.C.

_____ 11. The major Etruscan gods were similar to those of **Egypt**.

_____ 12. The Etruscans were an ancient people who lived in what is now central **Spain**.

_____ 13. The Etruscans had exceptional **harbors** that promoted trade.

_____ 14. The Etruscan language continued to be used by the Romans for some **business** ceremonies.

_____ 15. The **lucomon** was elected each year.

_____ 16. The Etruscan civilization was the first great civilization on the Italian **peninsula**.

_____ 17. The Etruscans did not have a strong central government, but a number of **city-states**.

_____ 18. The Etruscans were influenced by the **Persians**.

_____ 19. The Etruscans formed a **league** of 12 cities.

_____ 20. The Etruscans gave the **Phoenicians** the alphabet.

_____ 21. By the third century B.C., the Etruscan **culture** gradually disappeared.

_____ 22. The Etruscan alphabet is based on the **Egyptian** alphabet.

_____ 23. The Etruscans lived in the area Italians today call **Tuscaloosa**.

_____ 24. The Etruscan Culture stretched from Campania in the south to the **Po** Valley in the north.

_____ 25. Etruscan cities were often surrounded by **moats** for protection from attack.

The Celts

The Celts were people of Indo-European stock who first appeared in Central Europe in the eighth century B.C. They lived in the countries we now call Austria, the Czech Republic, Slovakia, Germany, Hungary, and Switzerland. They were the first people in Northern Europe to make iron. Iron tools made it possible for these early Celts to clear and farm more land than ever before. Larger farming areas resulted in more food, which resulted in an increased population. The increased population led to overcrowding; many of these early Celts left in search of fertile river valleys in which to settle. The Celts spread to France, Belgium, Portugal, Spain, and the British Isles. Some Celtic groups moved to what are now Bulgaria and Greece. Some even settled in Northern Italy.

By 500 B.C. the Celts had developed into a civilization. Unlike some civilizations, the Celts were not united under one leader. Their culture was divided into tribes, and each tribe was independent. Within each tribe, the Celts were split into three classes. There were the nobles or aristocrats, which included warriors; the Druids, or learned class, who were also noblemen; and the peasants or common people, which included farmers and craftsmen. Although these are the general groups within a Celtic tribe, members of one group would sometimes perform the functions of another.

Being some of the most skillful artisans of their time, the Celts created intricate gold and metal works that were prized throughout the civilized world. They primarily used local materials to make pottery, enamel work, and jewelry. They were also excellent farmers, herders, weavers, miners, and traders. One skill that was especially helpful was the Celts' ability to build roads. This skill made it possible for the Celts to expand their culture into other countries.

Celts were a puzzle to those from other civilizations. On the one hand, they were mean and ruthless warriors who often went into battle naked to show they were unafraid. They raided and looted, sacrificed humans, took slaves, and killed their enemies and collected their skulls. On the other hand, to those who were not their enemies, they were very friendly. For their time, they were uncommonly kind to the sick and old. There is evidence that in 300 B.C. some tribes had built and maintained a hospital to care for those who could not care for themselves.

The Celts were an artistic and musical people who loved the spoken word. Since they did not have a written language, their history and literature was memorized and passed down orally from generation to generation. Most of the culture's knowledge was preserved by the Druids who were priests who performed the duties of teachers, judges, and doctors.

While many respected the Celts, the Romans did not. They called them Gauls and considered the Celts a vulgar race of barbarians who loved war and made human sacrifices. Their hatred for the Celts and their lust for the land the Celts controlled made conflict between these two powers inevitable. About 390 B.C., the armies of the Celts and the Romans clashed, and the Celts won a decisive victory. The Celts went to Rome and looted it. The Celtic victory was short-lived, however. For the next several centuries, the Romans conquered most of Europe. The Celtic culture was greatly reduced and almost eliminated by the Romans and the Germanic people. The only traces of the Celtic culture that remain today are in the British Isles and in northwest France.

CELTIC CIVILIZATION AT A GLANCE

WHERE: Europe

WHEN: 800 B.C. TO A.D. 200

ACHIEVEMENTS:
- Skillful artisans
- Excellent farmers
- Fearless warriors
- Artistic and musical people
- Built roads to expand into other countries
- First people in Northern Europe to make iron

World Civilizations and Cultures

Ancient Europe: Why Did the Descendents of the Celts Leave Europe?

Name: _____ Date: _____

Why Did the Descendents of the Celts Leave Europe?

Since the largest group of people of Celtic ancestry living in the United States is Irish, many people in the United States think that Celtic means Irish. This is not true, but it is easy to understand this view since nearly two million descendents of the Celts came from Ireland to the United States during the 1840s and 1850s. These Irish people not only immigrated to the United States, they settled in Canada and other countries in order to begin a new life.

Do you know why so many Irish people wanted to leave Ireland and immigrated to the United States in the mid 1800s? The cause is a well-known disaster that Ireland experienced. If you solve the problem shown below, you will find out.

Each of the scrambled words below and to the left is important to the Celtic culture. Unscramble each word into its correct order and then place the letters in the boxes and circles to the right. When you are finished, if you read the words formed by the letters in the circles, you will discover why so many Irish immigrated to the United States in the 1800s.

1. npaesat

2. ueopre

3. fratc

4. sphtaoil

5. tool

6. inro

7. fmearr

8. riwaror

9. maron

10. dudir

11. brbaiaarn

12. etcl

Ancient Rome

Like the Greeks, Romans had myths, legends, and gods they used to explain the world, their history, and their heritage. One famous Roman legend explains how Rome was founded. According to the story, Rome was founded by Romulus and Remus, twin brothers who were the sons of Mars, the Roman god of war. Shortly after birth, a wicked relative tried to drown the twins by throwing them into the Tiber River. They were washed ashore, and a female wolf rescued them and fed them as if they were her own. The boys were found and raised by a shepherd and his wife. When the boys grew up, they founded Rome and then quarreled over who would be king. Romulus killed Remus and became the first of Rome's seven kings, reigning from 753 to 716 B.C.

Roman history can be divided into three periods: the Monarchy, the Republic, and the Empire.

THE MONARCHY

Rome was first ruled by kings, sometimes called **monarchs**. The city was governed by six kings after Romulus. During this period, the city grew, the Roman religion was established, and roads, aqueducts, and bridges were built. The last of the seven kings of this period was Tarquinius the Proud, a tyrant who was so hated, he was thrown out in 509 B.C. After Tarquinius was thrown out, the wealthy landowners in Rome established a Republic.

THE ROMAN REPUBLIC

A **republic** is a political system in which a group of citizens elects representatives and officers to run the government. A republic is sometimes a democracy. However, the one established in Rome was not a democracy because only powerful, wealthy families belonged to the senate.

The **senate** was the assembly of aristocratic families who elected or appointed many people to perform public jobs. The two most important people they appointed were called **consuls**. The consuls were given a great deal of authority to make decisions for Rome. When Rome had an extreme emergency, the senate could appoint a **dictator** to deal with the crisis.

The wealthy class in Rome was known as the **patricians**. **Plebeians** were the common people in Rome. They were the traders, workers, and peasants. While the Republic worked well for the patricians, who were able to make decisions in the senate, the plebeians felt they were no better off, since they could not hold office and had no voice in the government. The friction caused by this inequity continued until 493 B.C. when the plebeians were given representatives, called **tribunes**, in the senate. The plebeians were able to have the tribunes establish a set of protective laws.

ROMAN EMPIRE AT A GLANCE

WHERE: Italy

WHEN: 500 B.C.–A.D. 1453

ACHIEVEMENTS:

- United many people and established peace over a great area
- Established laws that served as a basis for legal systems for many countries
- Latin, its language, is the basis for many other languages such as Italian, French, Portuguese, and Spanish.
- Built magnificent structures such as the Colosseum and the Pantheon; their architects made extensive use of the dome and arch
- Built paved roads, bridges, and aqueducts to carry water
- Invented the numbering system called Roman numerals, which is still used
- Developed the Julian calendar, which is still used today
- Introduced concrete and road signs

In addition to the conflict between the patricians and the plebeians, the Roman Republic also had to deal with a series of wars with its neighbors. Fortunately, Rome had a large, strong army, a plentiful food supply, metals to make weapons, and slaves to do much of the work. Each war brought new power and new land under Roman domination. Eventually, the Romans controlled all of Italy and most of the land facing the Mediterranean Sea. Greece, part of Spain, and Gaul, now known as France, were all under Roman control. The main enemy of Rome was Carthage in North Africa. Rome and Carthage fought three wars called the Punic Wars over a hundred-year period.

Each new land acquired by the Romans became a **province**. The Romans signed a treaty with each defeated nation requiring them to pay taxes to Rome. In exchange, the important people of the conquered nation could become Roman citizens, vote in elections, and become elected to public office. Those who chose to become Roman citizens had to adopt a Roman name and wear Roman clothes. Even the conquered people who did not become citizens often adopted the Roman language and its customs.

THE ROMAN EMPIRE

Continued military victories made some Roman generals very powerful. Soldiers began to give their loyalty to the generals rather than to the senate or Rome. Some generals used this loyalty to try to become dictators and take power away from the senate. There was chaos in Rome. No one was able to stay in power for very long. In 46 B.C. Julius Caesar, a general and hero, became dictator.

Caesar accomplished many things in the short time he was dictator. He reduced taxes, built buildings, and reformed the calendar. The Julian calendar was named after him, and although there have been a few minor changes, it is still used today. The changes Caesar made in Rome improved the lives of the plebeians, so they liked him. His soldiers liked him too. However, the patricians did not like him because he had become too powerful. Several senators decided to kill him, and on March 15, 44 B.C., Caesar was assassinated.

Eventually, Caesar's adopted son, Octavian, assumed power and became the first **emperor** of Rome. He called himself Augustus, which means "great." This was the beginning of the Roman Empire. It is sometimes called the Age of Emperors or Rome's Golden Age. While consuls were still elected every year, the emperor was the absolute ruler.

Augustus was a good ruler. He kept peace, built roads and buildings, and encouraged the arts and sciences. He ruled from 27 B.C. until A.D. 14. After Augustus, there were other emperors, some better than others. There was peace, however, and the empire continued to grow. Although there were occasional rebellions against Roman rule, those conquered came to accept being part of the Roman Empire. In A.D. 212, the Emperor Caracalle decreed that all free men and women, including those who had previously been slaves, were Roman citizens. Slaves could not claim citizenship.

About A.D. 180, the Roman Empire began to decline. The Empire was so large that it was hard to manage. It was divided into two parts—the Latin Western Empire and the Greek Eastern Empire. The Greek Eastern Empire was also called the Byzantine Empire. Constantinople was the capital of the Greek Eastern Empire. It was named after the Emperor Constantine. The Eastern Empire was toppled in 1453 when the Turks conquered Constantinople. The Western Empire was invaded by various Germanic tribes and by Mongols called Huns. The Romans called these invaders barbarians, which meant they lived outside the empire. The fall of ancient Rome was complete. But many of its buildings, ideas of government, and remnants of its language exist today.

Map of the Roman Empire A.D. 117

The boundaries of the Roman Empire were Britain in the north, Egypt in the south, Spain in the west, and Syria in the east.

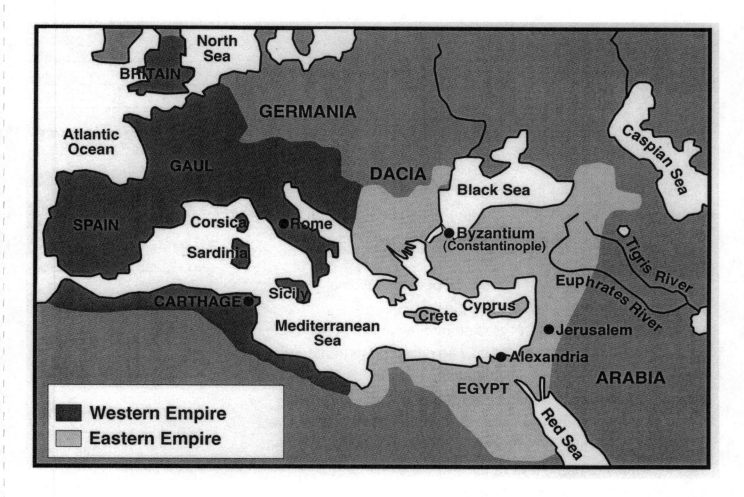

Name: _____   Date: _____

Roman Civilization Vocabulary

Below are a number of definitions dealing with Rome. In the blank after each definition, write the word that is described by the definition. The terms to be used are given at the bottom of the page.

DEFINITION	TERM
1. A ruler such as a king	_____
2. An area of a country located away from the capital	_____
3. The second longest river in Italy	_____
4. An ancient story dealing with supernatural beings or heroes	_____
5. An aristocrat	_____
6. Ruler of an empire	_____
7. An absolute ruler that Romans appointed to deal with a crisis	_____
8. Founded Rome with his brother in 753 B.C.; he was the first king	_____
9. A class of people considered superior to others	_____
10. The common people in Rome	_____
11. Representatives of the common people in Rome	_____
12. Government by all of the people	_____
13. One of the two leaders elected by the senate	_____
14. A structure like a bridge that was designed to transport water	_____
15. Many lands ruled by one country	_____
16. An assembly of Roman citizens who governed Rome	_____
17. A country ruled by an assembly of citizens instead of a king	_____
18. Three wars fought between Rome and Carthage	_____
19. The ancient name for France	_____
20. To murder for political reasons	_____
21. Primitive people; those who didn't live in the Roman Empire	_____
22. A large city in north Africa	_____
23. Another name for the Greek Eastern part of the Roman Empire	_____
24. The capital of the Greek Eastern Empire	_____
25. A country that is shaped like a boot	_____

Use these words:

Aristocracy, Assassinate, Barbarians, Byzantine, Carthage, Citizen, Constantinople, Consul, Democracy, Dictator, Empire, Emperor, Gaul, Italy, Myth, Patrician, Plebeian, Province, Punic, Republic, Romulus, Senate, Tiber, Tribune, Monarch

Name: _____ Date: _____

Make a Mosaic

Romans decorated their homes, courtyards, public buildings, and works of art with mosaics. Mosaics are pictures or designs made by setting small colored pieces of stone, tile, or glass into soft cement. Mosaics might be a simple geometric design or more elaborate pictures of fish, birds, animals, gods, or heroes. Mosaics are still used today. Here is your chance to design one.

Materials—Large sheet of heavy cardboard, sheet of paper, pencil, scissors, clay, modeling knife, paints, bowl, paintbrush, rolling pin, plaster of Paris, spreader, and sponge.

Step One—On a sheet of paper, create your design. A simple geometric design is the easiest. Animals, birds, fish, or objects such as bowls or pitchers are more difficult.

Step Two—Copy your design or picture onto the sheet of heavy cardboard.

Step Three—Roll out the clay until it is about $\frac{1}{8}$-inch thick. Using the ruler, cut the clay into squares. The size of the squares will depend on the size of your design. A square between $\frac{1}{4}$-inch and $\frac{1}{2}$-inch is ideal. A larger design will require large squares. A smaller design will require small squares. Smaller squares enable you to make more elaborate and intricate designs.

Step Four—After the tiles have dried, paint them different colors.

Step Five—When the paint has dried, decide which color you are going to use for each part of your design by placing the tiles directly on the design on the cardboard. You will need to move the tiles around to see what arrangement looks best. You may even decide to make some changes in your design to accommodate the tiles.

Step Six—Carefully spread the plaster of Paris on the cardboard, a little bit at a time. Press your tiles into place while the plaster of Paris is still wet. Since the plaster of Paris will cover your design as you apply it, is important that you put it on in small amounts. As you look at the part of the design that is not covered and the original drawing you did on your sheet of paper, you will be able to see where the tiles should be placed.

Step Seven—After the mosaic is dry, use a sponge or dry cloth to wipe away any residue from the plaster of Paris.

ALTERNATIVE METHOD OF MAKING A MOSAIC

While clay tiles placed on plaster of Paris gives a more authentic appearance of what ancient Roman mosaics looked like, you might choose a simpler, less authentic-looking method to make a mosaic.

Step One—Repeat steps one and two given above.

Step Two—Take four sheets of colored paper and cut them into squares of about $\frac{1}{8}$-inch.

Step Three—Spread glue over the design on the cardboard.

Step Four—Place the colored paper squares on your design.

Name: _____   Date: _____

The Calendar

The Romans used various calendars based on the sun, moon, and seasons. These calendars were also influenced by political and religious considerations, so they were not very accurate. When Caesar became dictator, the Roman calendar was in error by several months. Caesar asked Sosigenes, the astronomer, to help him reform the calendar so that it was accurate. Sosigenes created a calendar of 365 days and 6 hours. In order to make up for past errors so that the calendar would correspond with the seasons, the year 46 B.C. was given 445 days. After that, every year was to be based on the solar year, which is approximately 365 days and 6 hours. There were some changes later, but basically this Julian calendar is still in use today.

You may have wondered how the months of the year got their names. The name for each month has its roots in Rome. Shown below are the root words for the months. In the blank, write the modern name of the month taken from the Roman word. You should understand that the earliest Latin calendar had ten months, beginning with March. The 12-month calendar was developed during the reign of Julius Caesar. That is why it is called the Julian calendar.

ROOT WORD	MONTH
1. *Novem*, which means *nine*	_____
2. *Octo*, which means *eight*	_____
3. *Februare*, which means *to clean*	_____
4. *Decem,* which means *ten*	_____
5. *Augustus Caesar*, the Roman Emperor	_____
6. *Juno*, the Roman goddess	_____
7. *Mars*, the Roman god of war	_____
8. *Julius Caesar*, the Roman dictator	_____
9. *Janus*, the Roman god who was the doorkeeper of heaven	_____
10. *Septem*, which means *seven*	_____
11. *Maia*, the Roman goddess of spring	_____
12. *Aperire*, which means *to open*	_____

Name: _____   Date: _____

Planets and the Romans

Many ancient people worshipped the sun and moon and in some cases felt the planets were gods as well. Identifying planets with the major gods was common in religions in all parts of the world. These ancient people did not feel the planets represented the gods or were symbols of the gods, but they felt that the planets *were* the gods. They prayed to the planets and had ceremonies to honor them.

The planets, except for Earth, have been given names based on Roman mythology. Using the clues given below, figure out the names of the planets based on Roman mythology.

CLUES	PLANET

1. This planet is closest to the sun. The Romans named it after the Roman messenger to the gods because the planet appeared to move so fast. The Greek name is Hermes.   _____

2. This is the eighth planet from the sun. It was not known to the Romans but was seen in 1690 by John Flamsteed who thought it was a fixed star. In 1846, it was confirmed as a planet and named for the Roman god of the sea. The Greek name is Poseidon.   _____

3. This is the planet next to Earth. The Romans named it for their god of war because of its red, bloodlike color. It is sometimes called the red planet. The Greek name is Ares.   _____

4. The largest of the planets, it was named after the Romans' most important god. The Greek name was Zeus.   _____

5. This is the ringed planet. It was named for the Roman god of agriculture. This god was the father of Jupiter. The Greek name was Cronos, father of Zeus.   _____

6. Named for the Roman goddess of love and beauty, this planet was considered to be the brightest and most beautiful. Other civilizations named it for their god or goddess of love or war. It is the hottest planet. The Greek name is Aphrodite.   _____

7. This is the seventh planet from the sun. It was named for the Roman god of heaven and father of the Titans. The Greek name is the same as the Roman name.   _____

8. Discovered in 1930, this is the smallest of the planets and is named after the Roman god of the underworld. The Greek name is Hades.   _____

Name: _____   Date: _____

Latin is Alive and Well and Living in America

Many of the phrases we use in our language today are taken from the Latin language used by the Romans. Shown below are a list of definitions. In the blank, list the appropriate Latin term. Use the terms at the bottom of page 61.

DEFINITION	**TERM**
1. Made in good faith; authentic; sincere	_____
2. Pound	_____
3. Before noon	_____
4. And others	_____
5. Actually in power; in reality	_____
6. Someone unacceptable or unwelcome	_____
7. A no-contest plea in court instead of guilty or innocent	_____
8. For every hundred	_____
9. That is	_____
10. Master of Arts	_____
11. In the year of the Lord	_____
12. The material evidence in a homicide, such as the corpse	_____
13. It does not follow	_____
14. Bachelor of Arts	_____
15. After noon	_____
16. For the time being; temporarily	_____
17. A writ requiring that evidence of wrongdoing, including a person being detained, be brought before a judge	_____
18. To infinity; no end	_____
19. Spontaneously; without rehearsal	_____
20. Method of operating	_____
21. And so forth	_____
22. By the year	_____
23. For example	_____
24. Second self	_____
25. Written after; usually at the end of a letter	_____
26. Against	_____
27. The northern lights	_____
28. May he rest in peace	_____

Name: _____ Date: _____

29. A male graduate or former student of a school, college, or university _____

30. In absence _____

31. The existing condition _____

32. Agreement _____

33. To the point of nausea _____

34. Before the war _____

35. In memory of _____

36. The school, college, or university that one has attended _____

37. Let the buyer beware _____

38. After death _____

39. In reverse _____

40. Something for something _____

41. Horn of plenty _____

42. A writ requiring appearance in court to give testimony _____

43. With great praise _____

44. An addition _____

45. By the day _____

46. For every person _____

47. Solid earth _____

48. O come, all ye faithful _____

49. Factual information _____

50. All the courses of study offered by a school _____

Use these words and phrases:

(A.D.—Anno Domini)	addendum	Adeste Fideles	ad infinitum
ad nauseam	(ad lib., ad libitum)	alma mater	alter ego
alumnus	(A.M.—Ante Meridiem)	ante bellum	aurora borealis
(B.A.—Baccalaureus Artium)		bona fide	caveat emptor
consensus	cornucopia	corpus delicti	curriculum
data	de facto	et cetera	(et al.—et alii, et alia)
(e.g.—exempli gratia)	exit	habeas corpus	in absentia
(i.e.—id est)	in memoriam	(lb.—libra)	
(M.A.—Magister Artium)	magna cum laude	modus operandi	nolo contendere
non sequitur	per annum	per capita	
(per cent—per centum)	per diem	(P.M.—Post Meridiem)	
post mortem	(P.S.—post scriptum)	(pro tem—pro tempore)	
quid pro quo	(R.I.P.—requiescat in pace)		status quo
subpoena	terra firma	versus	vice versa

The Vikings

"The Vikings are coming! The Vikings are coming!" This is the dreaded alarm that spread terror throughout Europe from the late eighth to the 11th century A.D. The Vikings attacked and raided cities all across Europe, including London and Paris. Monasteries were the frequent targets of raids because that was often where a region's wealth was stored. The Vikings would raid a monastery, steal its treasures, kidnap the monks, and sell them as slaves in the East.

The key to the success of the Viking raids was surprise and swiftness. They often planned their attacks on Sunday when they knew the people and the monks would be in church. Their longships were very shallow, making it possible for them to sail right onto the beach or inland into the rivers, quickly get off their ship, raid the monastery, put their loot on the ship, and escape before the people could mount an organized defense.

The Vikings, which is a word that means "pirates," were not all ruthless soldiers plundering farms and monasteries. In fact, most Vikings lived peacefully. Originally known as Norsemen or Danes, the Vikings were hunters, farmers, fishermen, and craftsmen living in the Scandinavian countries we now call Norway, Denmark, and Sweden. They were excellent seamen, navigators, craftsmen, shipbuilders, traders, and great storytellers. We know a great deal of their history through stories of their adventures that are called **sagas**.

These sagas reveal that until the end of the eighth century, Vikings lived rather peaceful lives as farmers and fishermen. However, as the Viking population grew, the scarcity of land caused many Vikings to leave their homes and become seamen and soldiers. Some explored other lands and established settlements in places like Greenland, Iceland, England, Scotland, Spain, France, and Ireland. Some sailed into the Mediterranean, and others traveled to what is now America, centuries before Columbus. Others chose to raid towns and monasteries for treasures, food, and slaves.

To say that these raiding Vikings were feared would be an understatement. In fact the word *berserk* comes from the Viking word *berserkr* which meant "bear-shirt." A **berserker** was a brave warrior who would put on a bear skin prior to a battle and work himself into a frenzy to prepare for the fight. It is said that a berserker was a madman in battle, never feeling pain and killing many people. It was a great honor for a Viking to die in battle. Those who did were transported to Valhalla. The Vikings believed Valhalla was a paradise where the dead would enjoy themselves by fighting and feasting.

Perhaps the skills that made the Vikings unique were shipbuilding and sailing. While other Europeans kept close to shore when they sailed, Vikings crossed the Atlantic Ocean without a compass or other modern instruments. Archaeologists believe they were able to navigate these great distances by observing the sun, stars, and the different species of birds and sea animals they would see. They would even taste sea water as they were sailing. If the water was not too salty, they knew that land was close by, since fresh water empties into the ocean.

VIKING CIVILIZATION AT A GLANCE
WHERE: Scandinavian countries we now call Norway, Denmark, and Sweden
WHEN: Late eighth to 11th century A.D.
ACHIEVEMENTS:
• They were excellent seamen, navigators, craftsmen, shipbuilders, traders, explorers, and great storytellers.
• We know a great deal of their history through stories of their adventures that are called sagas.
• Many of the names of the days of the week are taken from the

The Vikings had different sizes of ships. One kind only held four men, while fighting ships, called **longships**, were up to 90 feet long and held 50 warriors. While their ships were built in different sizes, they were all designed in a similar manner. They were long, thin, and light with a curve at each end. They were flexible so they wouldn't break up on the rough ocean. A large, square sail moved the ship when the wind was strong enough. When it wasn't,

A Viking Longship

the men rowed. In bad weather, the sail was lowered and used as a tent to protect the sailors.

Their ships not only sailed well on the oceans, their special design made it possible for them to sail inland on rivers. They had a keel that cut through the water very fast and made the ship stable. The prow of a longship was carved into a menacing figure, such as a dragon, snake, or some other animal. They were very fast, and their rudders made them easy to maneuver.

A great deal of the Vikings' culture involved their ships. Not only were they important for raids, trading, and moving to new settlements, many rich Vikings were either buried or cremated in ships. These ships were stuffed with the deceased's belongings, such as weapons, household goods, furniture, food, and anything else they might need on their journey to the next world. Often horses, dogs, other animals, and sometimes slaves were sacrificed and placed aboard the ship. Ordinary people were sometimes buried in graves marked with stones in the shape of a boat.

The Vikings believed there were many gods who lived in Asgard. The main god was Odin or Wodan, the ruler of Valhalla. Valhalla was a hall in Asgard where dead warriors were brought back to life. Odin's son was Thor, the god of thunder and of law and order. Thor would throw his hammer at monsters and drive his chariot pulled by goats across the sky. When people heard the sound of thunder, they said it was Thor driving his chariot and throwing his hammer. Freya was a fertility goddess, and Tiu was a god of war.

The Vikings had three different classes of people—aristocrats, freemen, and slaves. The aristocrats were nobles and were called **jarls**. They owned land; they had farms, ships, and slaves. A jarl could eventually become a king of his region. Freemen were **karls**. They were free-born peasants and often owned land. Some were traders, craftsmen, or worked on farms owned by jarls or other karls. The slaves were **thralls**. They were prisoners of war or children whose parents were thralls. They did all of the unpleasant jobs. All freemen would attend open-air meetings called **things** to discuss problems and settle disputes.

The Viking influence is still with us today. Shown below are the origins of the days of the week. Many are taken from the Norse language.

Sunday: Day of the sun (Germanic)
Monday: Day of the moon (Germanic)
Tuesday: Day of Tiu or Tyr, the Norse god of war
Wednesday: Day of Odin or Woden, the chief Norse god
Thursday: Day of Thor, the Norse god of thunder
Friday: Day of Freya, the Norse goddess of love
Saturday: Day of Saturn, the Norse god Saturn

Name: _____ Date: _____

Viking Civilization Vocabulary

Below are a number of definitions dealing with the Vikings. In the blank after each definition, write the word from the list at the bottom of the page that is described by the definition.

DEFINITION	**TERM**
1. Destructive, violent, or extremely upset	_____
2. The word originally meant "pirates," but now refers to a group who lived in Scandinavia between the eighth and 11th centuries	_____
3. Stories of Viking adventures	_____
4. The main structure of a ship; runs lengthwise along the center line from bow to stern; the frames are attached to it	_____
5. A hall in Asgard; it is paradise to a Viking	_____
6. The forward part of a ship; the bow	_____
7. Many rich Vikings were either buried or cremated in these	_____
8. Vikings who were nobles	_____
9. To plan a route for and maneuver a ship or boat	_____
10. The day of the week named after the Viking god Tiu or Tyr	_____
11. Vikings believed there were many gods who lived in this place.	_____
12. The main Viking god who ruled Valhalla	_____
13. The day of the week named after the Viking goddess Freya	_____
14. The Viking god of war	_____
15. Freemen who often owned land; not aristocrats	_____
16. The Viking god of thunder	_____
17. The Viking fertility goddess	_____
18. Open-air meetings attended by freemen	_____
19. Slaves	_____
20. A warship	_____
21. Another name for Norway, Denmark, and Sweden	_____
22. A brave warrior who would put on a bear skin prior to a battle and would work himself into a frenzy to prepare for a battle	_____
23. This feature of the Viking ship made it easy to maneuver.	_____
24. The Vikings believed that these animals pulled Thor's chariot.	_____
25. The day of the week named after the Norse god Saturn	_____

Use these words: **Asgard, Berserk, Berserker, Freya, Friday, Goats, Jarls, Karls, Keel, Longship, Navigate, Odin, Prow, Rudder, Sagas, Saturday, Scandinavia, Ships, Things, Thor, Thralls, Tiu, Tuesday, Valhalla, Vikings**

The Middle East: The Phoenicians

The Phoenicians lived in small city-states along the Mediterranean coast in what is now Lebanon from about 2000 B.C. to 800 B.C. Two famous Phoenician cities are Tyre and Sidon. The people were originally Canaanites, but the Greeks named them Phoenicians. It is thought the name Phoenician comes from the Greek word *phoinikes,* meaning "purple men." The Greeks gave them that name because the Phoenicians developed the process of making purple dye. The dye was beautiful, but it was so expensive that only the wealthy could afford it. Roman emperors wore purple togas, and over time, the color purple became associated with royalty.

Dye was not the only Phoenician product that was prized throughout the Mediterranean. Fine glassware made into vases, bottles, goblets, and beads was treasured as well. The Phoenicians learned glassmaking from the Egyptians, but they improved the process. While Egyptian glass was cloudy, the Phoenicians used sand rich in quartz from their own country. The abundance of quartz in the sand made the Phoenician glass clear. Both clear and colored glassware made by Phoenician craftsmen were treasured objects. Beautiful ivory and wood carvings, pottery, cedar wood, wine, wrought metal objects, and embroidered cloth also made Phoenician traders wealthy.

By 1250 B.C., the Phoenicians had established themselves not only as excellent craftsmen and traders, but as outstanding navigators and sailors as well. Their sailing skill was developed as they looked for new markets and raw materials for their products. They sailed all over the Mediterranean world, and according to a Greek historian, may have even sailed around Africa, which would have been about 2,000 years before Europeans accomplished this feat. Phoenicians were among the first people to learn to sail at night by navigating by the stars.

The Phoenicians traded their goods with many nations and set up trading posts in many places in the Mediterranean. The most famous trading post was in Carthage in northern Africa, which became a power in the Mediterranean by the seventh century B.C. There were other important trading posts at Utica near Carthage, Cadiz in southern Spain, and on the islands of Cyprus and Rhodes. While Phoenicia had many posts and colonies in different places, it is not accurate to call Phoenicia an empire. All of the city-states in Phoenicia and the colonies in other countries were independent.

Perhaps the greatest accomplishment of the Phoenicians was the invention of the alphabet. Earlier civilizations had developed forms of writing based on pictures. While these were great advancements in communication, these writing systems were **pictographs**. The Phoenician **alphabet** was better because each symbol represented a sound. Since there are about 30 different sounds in speech, this means that any word can be written using a system of 30 letters or less. The Phoenician alphabet used 22 letters. Since the Phoenicians traveled to so many places, their alphabet spread to other countries. The Greeks adapted the Phoenician alphabet and called their first letter "alpha" and their second letter "beta." Combining these two letters gives us the word "alphabet." Today all modern languages are written with the alphabetic system.

PHOENICIAN CIVILIZATION AT A GLANCE

WHERE: West Asia

WHEN: 2000 B.C.–800 B.C.

ACHIEVEMENTS:
- Invented the alphabet and a writing system; most early writing systems were based on pictures
- The greatest traders of the ancient world
- Talented craftsmen known for their ivory carvings
- Developed the technique of glassblowing
- Excellent navigators, sailors, and shipbuilders.

Name: _____ Date: _____

Phoenician Civilization Quiz

Shown below are a number of sentences. Some are true and some are false. If the sentence is true, write "true" in front of the sentence. If the sentence is false, write a term that could replace the word in bold type to make the sentence true.

_____ 1. Phoenician glass was **opaque**.

_____ 2. The Phoenicians developed the process of making a **purple** dye.

_____ 3. Two famous Phoenician **kings** were Tyre and Sidon.

_____ 4. Over time, the color purple became associated with **peasants**.

_____ 5. The Phoenicians' greatest accomplishment was the invention of the **rudder**.

_____ 6. Phoenician **sailing** skill was developed as they looked for new markets and raw materials for their products.

_____ 7. The Phoenician purple dye was beautiful and **cheap**.

_____ 8. In the Phoenician alphabet, each symbol represented a **syllable**.

_____ 9. Pictographs are writing systems using **sounds** to represent ideas.

_____ 10. Phoenicians were originally called the **Sumerians**.

_____ 11. Phoenicians were excellent **navigators**.

_____ 12. It is not accurate to call the Phoenician culture an **empire**.

_____ 13. Phoenician comes from a Greek word meaning "**bearded men**."

_____ 14. Phoenicians lived in city-states along the **Mediterranean** coast.

_____ 15. The Phoenicians learned glassmaking from the **Venetians**.

_____ 16. The **Romans** named the Canaanites "Phoenicians."

_____ 17. The Phoenicians had important **forts** at Utica near Carthage, Cadiz in southern Spain, and on Cyprus and Rhodes.

_____ 18. **Dye** from Phoenicia was prized throughout the Mediterranean.

_____ 19. The Phoenician culture existed from about **2000 to 800 B.C.**

_____ 20. Sand from Phoenicia was rich in **coral**.

_____ 21. The Phoenicians **marched** all over the Mediterranean world.

_____ 22. Phoenicia had many **posts** and **colonies** in foreign countries.

_____ 23. Phoenician city-states and the colonies were **independent**.

_____ 24. The Phoenician traders were **healthy**.

_____ 25. Phoenicians were among the first to navigate by the **compass**.

The Hebrews

The Hebrews were a nomadic group of Semitic people who originally came from Mesopotamia about 2000 B.C. and settled in an area close to the Mediterranean Sea in the Middle East. Most of the migration occurred between the 14th and 12th centuries B.C. Hebrews, the ancestors of today's Jews, called the area where they settled Israel. About the same time as the Hebrews were settling this area, the Philistines arrived. The name "Palestine" is based on their name. The descendants of the Philistines are the Arabs, some Muslims, and some Christians.

Some of the Hebrews moved to Egypt in search of more fertile land. When new pharaohs came to power in Egypt, they made the Israelites slaves. Moses, who was from Hebrew descent but lived in Egypt, was successful in getting the Israelites released from their bondage. Moses led the Hebrews out of Egypt and eventually into Canaan. Their escape from Egypt is known as the Exodus, which means "to leave." Joshua, Moses's successor, led the Hebrews as they regained Palestine and made Jerusalem their capital.

An important element of the Hebrew culture was its religion. The Hebrew religion was much different than other civilizations in the region. Hebrews developed the idea of **monotheism**, which means they believed there was only one god. Most other cultures believed the world was created and ruled by many gods; this philosophy is called **polytheism**. The Hebrews believed that the God who created the world also controlled the world. They believed that people could talk to God through prayer. They also believed that the image of God should not be made into a statue and worshipped. Many of these beliefs were radical at the time.

Their laws also set the Hebrews apart. In most cultures, the king was the ruler, and he made the laws that everyone had to obey. The laws under a king could be changed as easily as the king changed his mind. Other cultures developed strict laws whose only purpose was to keep some kind of order in the society. Often, these laws were only for common people. Kings and noblemen did not have to obey them. The Hebrews, however, had a set of laws based on their religion, and they applied them to everyone, including the rulers. Their laws, called the "Ten Commandments," are found in Exodus in the Old Testament of the *Bible.*

The Old Testament, written between 1200 B.C. and 150 B.C., tells the Hebrew history. It tells how the Hebrew tribes rose to power in Palestine led by kings Saul, David, and Solomon. It tells how the kingdom eventually split into two small states, Israel and Judah, and how these states were eventually destroyed. Israel was conquered by Assyria in 721 B.C. Judah was conquered by Babylonia in 587 B.C. Palestine has been controlled by several foreign powers. Some of them are the Persians, Alexander the Great, the Hellenistic Ptolemies, and the Romans.

Three major religions developed in Jerusalem. They are **Judaism**, which is the Jewish religion; **Christianity**, developed by the followers of Jesus Christ; and **Islam**, which is followed in the Moslem world.

HEBREW CIVILIZATION AT A GLANCE

WHERE: The Middle East

WHEN: 2000 B.C.–30 B.C.

ACHIEVEMENTS:

- Believed in one god
- Established a set of moral laws called the "Ten Commandments"
- Their religious beliefs strongly influenced many modern-day religions
- Recorded their history, laws, and beliefs in the Old Testament

---

Hebrew Civilization Quiz

Shown below are a number of sentences. Some are true and some are false. If the sentence is true, write "true" in front of the sentence. If the sentence is false, write a term that could replace the word in bold type to make the sentence true.

_____ 1. The Hebrew escape from Egypt is known as the **Genesis**.

_____ 2. The Hebrews were a **nomadic** group of Semitic people.

_____ 3. **Saul** led the Hebrews out of Egypt.

_____ 4. **Monotheism** is the belief in only one god.

_____ 5. **Polytheism** is the belief in more than one god.

_____ 6. **Damascus** was the capital of the Hebrews.

_____ 7. Hebrews believed that the image of God should not be made into a **statue** and worshipped.

_____ 8. The Hebrews originally came from **Palestine** about 2000 B.C.

_____ 9. About the same time as the Hebrews were settling this area, the **Philistines** arrived.

_____ 10. Hebrews believed that people could talk to God through **priest-kings**.

_____ 11. Hebrews are the ancestors of today's **Jews**.

_____ 12. Hebrews called the area where they settled **Jericho**.

_____ 13. Palestine is based on the name of the **Philistines**.

_____ 14. The Israelites were enslaved by the **Greeks**.

_____ 15. The Hebrews had a set of laws based on their **religion**.

_____ 16. The **Ten Commandments** are part of the Hebrews' laws.

_____ 17. The **New Testament** of the *Bible* tells the history of the Hebrews.

_____ 18. **Judaism** is the Jewish religion.

_____ 19. **Christianity** was developed by followers of Jesus Christ.

_____ 20. **Islam** is followed in the Moslem world.

_____ 21. Judah was conquered by **Macedonia** in 587 B.C.

_____ 22. Israel was conquered by **Sumeria** in 721 B.C.

_____ 23. Israel eventually split into two small states, Israel and **Judah**.

_____ 24. Palestine has been controlled by Persians, Greeks, and **Chinese**.

_____ 25. The decendants of the Philistines include the Arabs, some **Muslims**, and some Christians.

The Persians

The Persian Empire was located east of the Fertile Crescent on the east side of the Persian Gulf. It was the largest empire the ancient world had known. Persia occupied land that is presently Iran and Afghanistan. Persians were not Semitic as many of the early civilizations in that part of the world had been. They were Indo-European and called themselves **Aryans**. The name Iran is based on the name Aryan.

The Persians and the Medes came to this area about 1300 B.C. The Medes were warriors who raided cities and caravans. In 550 B.C., Cyrus the Great, a Persian province ruler, led an army to defeat the Medes. Cyrus united the Medes and the Persians into a strong army to expand his kingdom.

Cyrus and his army were very successful. In only 15 years, his army of archers and cavalry-men conquered almost all of the ancient world. This included Asia Minor, the Fertile Crescent, the Indus Valley, and Egypt. The Persians treated those they defeated fairly and kindly. In fact, there is some evidence that when the Babylonians were defeated by the Persians, many Babylonians welcomed the Persians because they were unhappy with their own king. Cyrus freed the Jewish captives and led them back to Jerusalem. The Persians allowed the kingdoms they defeated to maintain their own cultures rather than to impose the Persian culture on them. Conquered people did, however, have to pay tribute to Persia. Cyrus was killed in battle in 530 B.C.

The Persian Empire gained prominence under the leadership of Darius I, who ruled from 522 B.C. to 486 B.C. The kingdom thrived. One of the qualities that made Darius a great leader was that he was a very good administrator and organizer. Since the Persian Empire was so large, the challenge was to maintain the lands it had acquired and to govern them. Darius divided this enormous empire into 20 provinces called **satrapies**. Each of these satrapies was managed by a governor called a **satrap**. Other leaders, such as judges and tax collectors, were Persians appointed by the emperor. The emperor also had an inspector who would visit the satrapies unannounced to make sure the officials were doing their jobs well and being loyal to the emperor. The Persians connected their empire with well-paved roads, which encouraged international trade.

One contribution of the Persians was the religion called **Zoroastrianism**. Zoroaster was a Persian prophet who had seven visions. These visions served as the basis for the religion called Zoroastrianism. Zoroastrianism became the official religion of the Persian empire and flourished for many years. It is still practiced in some places today. The *Avesta,* the Persian Bible, based on the views of Zoroaster, teaches that there is one supreme god who made the world, sun, moon, and stars. Everything that is good in the world was created by this powerful god. His name is Ahura Mazda. He was the god of life. Another god, Ahriman, created everything that was evil and bad. He was the god of death.

Persia fought several wars with the Greeks. The Persian Empire, which is sometimes called the Achaemenid Empire, lasted until 330 B.C. when it was conquered by Alexander the Great.

PERSIAN CIVILIZATION AT A GLANCE

WHERE: East of the Fertile Crescent in the Middle East

WHEN: 550 B.C.–330 B.C.

ACHIEVEMENTS:

- Built roads and canals
- Divided the empire into provinces so that it could be governed better
- Wrote the *Avesta,* the Persian Bible, based on the views of Zoroaster, a prophet
- Did not invent coinage, but were the first to put it to wide use

Name: _____   Date: _____

Persian Civilization Quiz

Fill in the following sentences with the appropriate word or words.

1. In only _____ years, Cyrus's army conquered almost all of the ancient world.
2. The _____ kingdom included Asia Minor, the Fertile Crescent, the Indus Valley, and Egypt.
3. Many _____ welcomed the Persians because they were unhappy with their king.
4. When the Persians conquered Babylon, their first act was to free the _____ captives and lead them back to _____ .
5. The Persians allowed the kingdoms they defeated to maintain their own _____ .
6. _____ was killed in battle in 530 B.C.
7. The Persians treated those they defeated _____ and _____ .
8. The Persian Empire gained prominence under the leadership of _____ .
9. The name _____ is based on the name Aryan.
10. Persia occupied land that is presently _____ and _____ .
11. The Persians were Indo- _____ .
12. Conquered kingdoms were required to pay _____ to Persia.
13. In the Zoroastrian religion, _____ is the god of life.
14. In the Zoroastrian religion, _____ is the god of death.
15. In 550 B.C., Cyrus the Great led an army to defeat the _____ .
16. The Persian Empire was located east of the _____ .
17. _____ was the largest empire the ancient world had known.
18. Persians called themselves _____ .
19. Judges and tax collectors were Persians appointed by the _____ .
20. Darius divided this enormous empire into 20 provinces called _____ .
21. Each satrapy was managed by a governor called a _____ .
22. Persia fought several wars with the _____ .
23. _____ was a Persian prophet.
24. The emperor had an _____ who would visit the satrapies to make sure the officials were doing their jobs well and being loyal to the emperor.
25. The _____ is the Persian Bible.
26. The Persian empire built well-paved roads, which encouraged international _____ .
27. One contribution of the Persians was the religion called _____ .
28. Persia was conquered by _____ in 330 B.C.
29. The Persian Empire is sometimes called the _____ Empire.
30. Zoroaster is said to have had _____ visions.

Name: _____   Date: _____

Persian Empire Map Activity

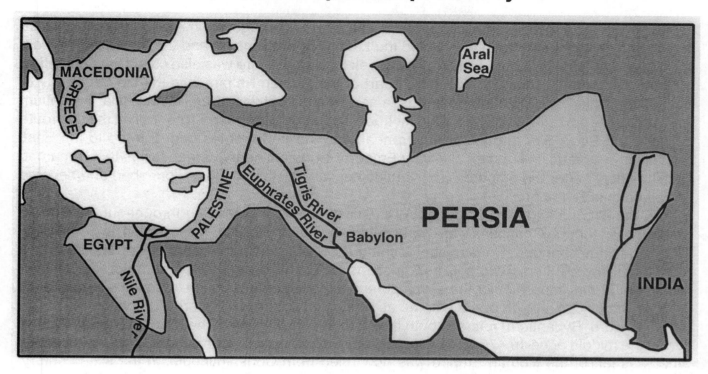

On the map of the Persian Empire shown above, find and label:

The Mediterranean Sea   **The Black Sea**   **The Red Sea**
The Caspian Sea   **The Persian Gulf**   **The Arabian Sea**
The Sahara Desert   **Crete**   **Cyprus**

Write a paragraph describing the difficulties involved in ruling a large empire, such as the Persian Empire.

_____

_____

_____

_____

_____

_____

_____

_____

The Byzantine Empire

The Roman Empire was so large that it was hard to manage, so in A.D. 395, it was divided in two. The section in the west was called the Latin Western Empire, and the section in the east was called the Greek Eastern Empire. The Greek Eastern Empire was also called the **Byzantine Empire**. The center of the Greek Eastern part of the Roman Empire was the old Greek city of Byzantium, which straddled the Bosporus, a narrow strait between Europe and Asia. Byzantium was a valuable port strategically located for trade and military purposes. It controlled the sea route between the Black Sea and the Mediterranean and the trade routes from Europe to the East. Byzantium was rebuilt as a capital city by Emperor Constantine the Great. It was then renamed Constantinople after the emperor. Constantinople, called Istanbul today, flourished and became as splendid as Rome.

In the second and third centuries A.D., Christianity was spreading throughout the Roman Empire, even though Christians were persecuted and put to death for their religion. In Byzantium, however, things changed. Constantine became a Christian after he had a vision. He issued an order that allowed others to worship as Christians. He eventually encouraged the spread of Christianity, which was important for the development of the Byzantine Empire. Gradually, Christianity became the official religion of the empire, as well as for medieval western Europe.

The word "Byzantium" refers to both the state and the culture of the Eastern Roman Empire during the middle ages. In 476, the Latin Western Empire was conquered by Germanic invaders. What was left of the Roman Empire was now ruled from Constantinople. In the sixth century, the Byzantine Empire stretched from southern Spain in the West to the borders of Sassanian Iran in the East. The Byzantine Empire was a diverse culture that combined many ethnic groups, languages, religions, and creeds. The Byzantines considered themselves Romans and faithfully maintained many of the traditions of Rome and Greece. When the Arabs conquered Egypt and Syria in 634, Byzantium changed. It became more Greek and less Roman. The Romans living in the Latin Western part of the Roman Empire did not regard those living in the Greek Eastern part very highly.

Byzantium was known for its art. Art created during this period is called Byzantine. Architecture, mosaics, enamel work, ivory carving, and metal work were all forms of art that developed in new and distinctive ways. Many of the works of art were created for altars of churches and imperial courts. One of the great architectural achievements of Byzantium was the construction of the church of Hagia Sophia, also known as Saint Sophia. It was built in Constantinople between A.D. 532 and 537. Today it is a mosque used by Moslems.

When the Ottomans seized power by the end of the sixth century, the Empire was being squeezed from all sides. The empire began to shrink as Arabs, Avars, Persians, Slavs, and Turks all conquered parts of Byzantium. By 1453, all that was left of the Byzantine Empire was

---

BYZANTINE CIVILIZATION AT A GLANCE

WHERE: Europe—The eastern section of the Roman Empire

WHEN: A.D. 500–1450

ACHIEVEMENTS:
- Preserved Greek and Roman culture and law
- Produced great works of art including architecture, mosaics, enamel work, ivory carving, and metal work
- Lasted almost 1,000 years
- Spread of Christianity

72

Constantinople. In May of that year, the Ottoman Turks captured the city and changed the name of Constantinople to Istanbul.

The loss of Constantinople to the Ottoman Empire was devastating to Western Europe. It was not only the end of Roman history and Christian power in the Eastern Mediterranean, it meant the Ottomans dominated trade through this important area.

The Byzantine Empire set a standard of cultural excellence for both halves of the Roman Empire. The results of the cultural development of the Byzantine Empire during these centuries has had a lasting impact on modern nations.

The Byzantine Empire Map

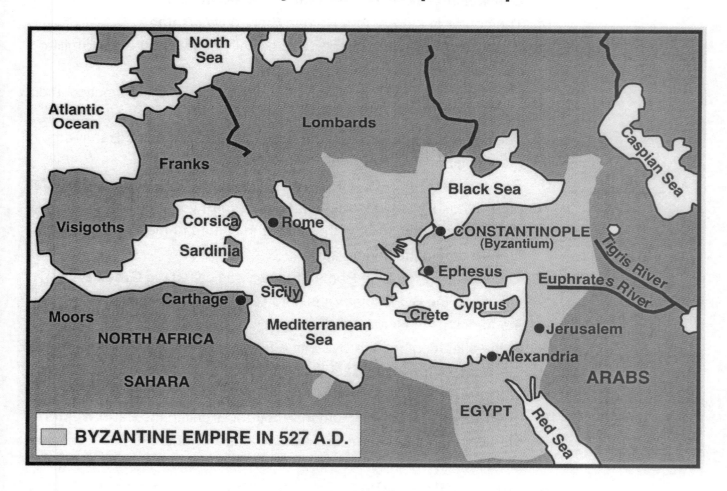

BYZANTINE EMPIRE IN 527 A.D.

73

Byzantine Empire Quiz

Shown below are a number of sentences. Some are true and some are false. If the sentence is true, write "true" in front of the sentence. If the sentence is false, write a term that could replace the word in bold type to make the sentence true.

_____ 1. The **Arabs** conquered Egypt and Syria in 634.

_____ 2. **Christians** were persecuted and put to death in Rome in the second and third centuries A.D.

_____ 3. Today Constantinople, which flourished, is called **Ephesus**.

_____ 4. **Judaism** became the official religion of the Byzantine Empire.

_____ 5. Constantinople was named for the Emperor **Noble**.

_____ 6. The center of the Eastern Roman Empire was **Rome**.

_____ 7. **Byzantium** was a valuable port strategically located for trade and military purposes.

_____ 8. Constantine issued an order allowing **Christians** to practice their religion.

_____ 9. The Byzantine Empire was a **diverse** culture that combined many ethnic groups, languages, religions, and creeds.

_____ 10. Romans living in the Latin Western part of the Roman Empire did not regard those living in the **Greek Eastern** part very highly.

_____ 11. **Byzantium** refers to both the state and culture of the Eastern Roman Empire during the middle ages.

_____ 12. The eastern part of the Roman Empire was called the **Greek Eastern**.

_____ 13. Originally, the Byzantines considered themselves **Greeks** and followed the traditions of Rome and Greece.

_____ 14. In the sixth century, the Byzantine Empire stretched from **England** in the West to Iran in the East.

_____ 15. **Gibraltar** is a narrow strait between Europe and Asia.

_____ 16. The western part of the Roman Empire was called the **Latin Western**.

_____ 17. Many works of **art** were created for altars of churches and imperial courts.

_____ 18. The loss of **Baghdad** to the Ottoman Empire was devastating to Western Europe.

_____ 19. One of the great architectural achievements of Byzantium was construction of the church of **Hagia Sophia**, also known as Saint Sophia.

_____ 20. In 1453, the Ottoman **Greeks** captured Constantinople.

The Muslim and Ottoman Empires

While the Byzantine Empire was thriving, a new religion, founded by a prophet named Muhammad, originated in Arabia in the seventh century A.D. The people who lived in Arabia were called **Arabs**. This new religion was called **Islam**, and those who belonged to this religion were called **Muslims**. Islam means "surrender to the will of Allah." *Allah* is the Arabic name for God. The Muslims felt their religion was the only true religion and that it was their duty to tell everyone.

Under the leadership of Muhammad, the Muslim Empire began to grow and take land from the Persian Empire and the Byzantine Empire. The first capital of the Muslim Empire was Damascus, the present capital of Syria. Baghdad, the present capital of Iraq, later became its capital. Although Muhammad died in 632, the empire expanded, and by the eighth century, it extended from Spain to India.

As the empire expanded, millions of the conquered people became Muslims. However, many Christians and Jews refused to give up their own faith. Although Muslim rulers, called **caliphs**, did not force people to accept their faith, those that did become Muslims paid lower taxes and were given other benefits.

The Muslim Empire began to decline and was divided into several independent kingdoms. Eventually, the Turks, under their leader Seljuk, conquered most of the Near East. In 1258, the Seljuk Turks were defeated by the Mongols.

The Ottomans were descendants of Turks who were originally mercenary soldiers of the Seljuks. They took over the old Seljuk states and established a new Muslim Empire called the Ottoman Empire. The Ottoman Empire was named after their leader, Osman I. For almost 700 years the empire was ruled by the descendants of Osman. The empire was located in northwestern Anatolia next to the Byzantine Empire.

The Ottomans felt it was their duty to defend their religion against those who were not Muslims. Osman, together with his son, Orkhan, conquered most of the Byzantine Empire by fighting a number of **jihads**, which are holy wars. Eventually, their empire expanded around Constantinople. However Osman and Orkhan were never able to capture Constantinople. Orkhan became sultan of the Ottoman Empire. *Sultan* is the Turkish name for "emperor." Constantinople was finally captured in 1453 by Mehmet II who was called the Conqueror. He ordered the largest Christian church, the Hagia Sophia, to become a **mosque**, a place where Muslims worship.

The empire expanded and reached its greatest power under Suleiman the Magnificent who ruled from 1520 to 1566. During his reign, the Ottomans conquered the Balkans, southern Russia, and northern Africa so that the empire now included much of eastern Europe and western Asia. Suleiman's accomplishments were not all military, however. He had mosques, monuments, bridges, roads, and schools built and also encouraged the arts and sciences.

The empire became weaker during the 18th and 19th centuries and came to an end after the First World War in 1923.

MUSLIM AND OTTOMAN EMPIRES AT A GLANCE

WHERE: The Near East, Balkans, Southern Russia, and Northern Africa

WHEN: A.D. 800–1923

ACHIEVEMENTS:

- Built many libraries, mosques, and schools
- Produced many great literary works
- Advanced the study of mathematics
- Developed and spread the Muslim religion
- Performed surgery and used chemicals to make medicine

Name: _____   Date: _____

Muslim and Ottoman Empires Quiz

Fill in the following sentences with the appropriate word or words.

1. Once the capital of the Muslim Empire, _____ is the present capital of Syria.

2. _____ is the Arabic name for God.

3. The people who lived in Arabia were called _____ .

4. The Ottoman Empire was named after their leader, _____ .

5. A prophet called _____ began a religion called Islam; he died in 632.

6. The Ottomans were descendants of _____ .

7. In 1258, the Seljuks were defeated by the _____ .

8. Osman's son was named _____ .

9. Muslim rulers were called _____ .

10. The _____ Empire lasted until the end of the First World War in 1923.

11. _____ means "surrender to the will of Allah".

12. The _____ Empire was in northwestern Anatolia, next to the Byzantine Empire.

13. _____ are holy wars.

14. _____ is the Turkish name for "emperor."

15. _____ was finally captured in 1453 by Mehmet II.

16. Mehmet II was called "_____ ."

17. The Muslim Empire took land from the _____ and the _____ Empires.

18. The _____ under their leader Seljuk, conquered most of the Near East.

19. Those who practice Islam are called _____ .

20. Those who were conquered by the Muslims and who did not convert to Islam were required to pay higher _____ .

21. The _____ felt it was their duty to defend their religion against those who were not Muslims.

22. Constantinople was renamed _____ .

23. The largest Christian church in Constantinople was the _____ .

24. Mehmet II decreed that this church become a _____ .

25. The Ottomans conquered the _____ Empire by 1453.

Name: _____ Date: _____

Three World Religions

   There were three religions widely practiced during the time of the Ottoman Empire, and they are still practiced today. They are Judaism, Christianity, and Islam. These three monotheistic religions count half the world's population as followers. Listed below are statements that relate to either Judaism, Christianity, or Islam. Before each statement are the letters "J," which represents Judaism, "C," which represents Christianity, and "I," which represents Islam. Circle the letter to which the statement refers. Some statements may refer to more than one religion. You may have to do some research to find the answers.

J C I 1. Their holy book is called the *Koran*

J C I 2. The oldest religion of the three

J C I 3. Considers Jerusalem a holy city

J C I 4. Celebrates the holy month of Ramadan

J C I 5. The official religion of the Ottoman Empire

J C I 6. This religion was divided in the 16th century by the Reformation

J C I 7. The first religion to teach monotheism, or belief in one god

J C I 8. Place of worship is a church

J C I 9. Considers Jesus to be the Messiah promised by God in the Old Testament

J C I 10. Uses the term "kosher" to apply to food that may be eaten

J C I 11. Must pray five times a day

J C I 12. Awaits the second coming of Christ

J C I 13. The Sabbath is observed by refraining from work and by attending a synagogue

J C I 14. Place of worship is a mosque

J C I 15. Celebrates Christmas

J C I 16. Celebrates Passover

J C I 17. Place of worship is a synagogue

J C I 18. Must make a pilgrimage to Mecca at least once, if at all possible

J C I 19. Their holy book is called the *Bible*

J C I 20. Their holy book is called the *Torah*

J C I 21. Celebrates Easter

J C I 22. Worships Allah

J C I 23. Became the official religion of Rome in the fourth century

J C I 24. Recognizes Muhammad as the prophet of Allah

J C I 25. Abraham, Isaac, and Jacob are considered patriarchs of this religion

Africa

KUSH

When one thinks of great civilizations or cultures in Africa, the name that leaps immediately to mind is Egypt. Egypt was an early, powerful, and important civilization that contributed a great deal to the development of the civilizations that followed. What many don't know is that there were other important civilizations that existed in Africa. This should not surprise anyone, since archae-ologists claim the earliest humans lived in East Africa. Africa may well be the cradle of all humanity.

About 12,000 years ago, the area we now call the Sahara Desert was not a desert at all, but a fertile area. Lush vegetation extended across the continent. Within this rich area, humans lived who fished, hunted, and gathered. Eventually, they began to herd animals and farm. While the Egyptian culture flourished between 3100 B.C. and 332 B.C., civilizations to the south and to the west of Egypt were just beginning to develop. While they were quite different from what most people think of as "civilization," nevertheless, the cultures that developed in Africa had music, art, and an oral history. They also traded gold, silver, copper, and ivory. One important African culture was known as the Kush.

The **Kush Civilization** was a very old civilization just south of Egypt along the Nile River. It was in an area we now call Sudan. The Kush Civilization began about 2000 B.C. and lasted until A.D. 350. The people of Kush were mainly fishermen and farmers. There were some tradesmen and some who built and sailed boats. The Egyptians were stronger than the Kush. They conquered them and took their precious metals, cattle, and ivory. They also enslaved them and took them back to Egypt. Eventually, the Kush grew stronger, and the Egyptians grew weaker. About 752 B.C. the Kush conquered the Egyptians, and for about a century, Kush kings governed Egypt.

The Kush ruled Egypt until they were conquered by the Assyrians who had iron weapons. Their defeat did not end the Kush civilization, however. They relocated their capital to Meroe and became a powerful culture. They mined and forged weapons and tools out of iron and spread their knowledge of iron-making to other parts of Africa. They developed a writing system, created art, and domesticated elephants. About A.D. 350, they were defeated by the Axum army.

GHANA

On the opposite side of the continent in West Africa, several kingdoms developed. The first of these West African empires was **Ghana**. Ghana was originally bordered on the west by the Senegal River, on the east by the Niger River, on the north by the Sahara Desert, and on the south by the jungle. It was this location that enabled Ghana to become rich and powerful. Although Ghana did not have as many resources as others in Africa, it was able to control the roads and charge taxes on caravans passing through the kingdom. The main items traded in this area were iron, gold, and salt.

AFRICAN EMPIRES AT A GLANCE

WHERE: Africa

WHEN: 2000 B.C. to present

ACHIEVEMENTS:

- Archaeological evidence shows this is where humans first lived.
- Kushites spread the knowledge of iron-making to other parts of Africa.
- Ghana controlled the gold and salt trade, established vital trade routes, and became wealthy by controlling trade routes and charging taxes.
- Zimbabweans were excellent builders who built a great walled city.

Ghana was a center for the iron industry. Its people made and traded iron weapons. Large numbers of warriors with iron weapons not only expanded the kingdom, but provided order to enable other tribes to trade and prosper. Although Ghana did have some gold, the area to the south of them had much more, and Ghana was able to control its trade. It is estimated that between the years A.D. 450 and 1230, more gold was traded in Ghana than at any other place in the world. While not as glamourous as gold, salt was also an important commodity in this era. Salt, which was mined in the Sahara Desert, was highly prized for its ability to preserve food.

The Ghana Kingdom became prominent around the eighth century, but flourished during the 10th and 11th centuries. Around 1200, when its kingdom extended from central Senegal to Timbuktu, Ghana's capital, Koumbi, was conquered by Berber Muslims. The kingdom of **Mali** followed the kingdom of Ghana. Mali included the area that once was Ghana, but it was larger.

ZIMBABWE

The city of Great Zimbabwe was located between the Zambeizi and the Limpopo Rivers. **Zimbabwe**, which means "great stone houses," was settled by Bantu-speaking people in about the year A.D. 600. Those living in Zimbabwe mined gold and copper and began trading it with people in Asia. Between 950 and 1450, Zimbabwe became important as a religious center. It was trade, however, that created great wealth in the 12th century and enabled the Zimbabweans to begin a building period that lasted several centuries. While African buildings were usually made from mud-brick, Great Zimbabwe is an exception. A huge stone wall was constructed to enclose the city. Inside the city, other walls were built to separate one area from another.

While it took several centuries to build the wall surrounding the Great Zimbabwe, when it was finished, the structure was among the most impressive created during the iron age in Africa. The massive stone walls are spread over an area of about 60 acres. What makes them most remarkable is not only their size—they were sixteen feet thick at the bottom and were 35 feet high—but the fact that the granite bricks were cut and shaped so precisely that mortar or cement was not needed to hold them in place.

The Great Zimbabwe enclosure was eventually abandoned, and it was destroyed by invaders. Today, only ruins remain of these once elaborate structures. The Zimbabwe Empire lasted until the 19th century. The Africans living in this region are so respectful of their ancestors and the magnificent structures they created that when they gained their independence in 1980, they named their country Zimbabwe.

The city of Great Zimbabwe

Name: _____   Date: _____

African Civilizations Quiz

Fill in the following sentences with the appropriate word or words.

1. For about a century, _____ kings governed Egypt.

2. _____ was a center for the iron industry.

3. _____ was a religious and trading center.

4. The Kush civilization was just south of Egypt, along the _____ River.

5. The Great _____ covered an area of about 60 acres.

6. Ghana was conquered by _____ Muslims.

7. It took several centuries to build the _____ surrounding Great Zimbabwe.

8. The Assyrians defeated the Egyptians because they had _____ weapons.

9. Ghana's capital was _____ .

10. Zimbabwe means "great _____ houses."

11. About 12,000 years ago, the _____ Desert was not a desert.

12. The walls of Great Zimbabwe were _____ feet thick and were _____ feet high.

13. People of Ghana controlled the roads and charged _____ on caravans.

14. _____ included the area that once was Ghana, but it was larger.

15. The Zimbabwe Empire lasted until the _____ century.

16. _____ is considered by some to be the cradle of all humanity.

17. Those living in Zimbabwe gained their _____ in 1980.

18. Ghana was in _____ Africa.

19. African buildings were usually made from _____ .

20. The Great Zimbabwe was made of _____ bricks.

21. Egypt was an important _____ civilization.

22. The Great Zimbabwe enclosure was eventually destroyed by _____ .

23. The _____ took precious metals, cattle, and ivory when they conquered the Kush.

24. The Kush ruled Egypt until they were conquered by the _____ .

25. The people of Kush were mainly fishermen and _____ .

26. _____ , used to preserve food, was mined in the Sahara Desert.

27. Between 450 and 1230, more gold was traded in _____ than at any other place.

28. The Kush Civilization relocated its capital to _____ .

29. The Kush Civilization was located in an area we now call _____ .

30. The Great Zimbabwe was located between the Zambeizi and the Limpopo _____ .

Name: _____ Date: _____

African Map Activity

Shown below is a map of Africa. Identify and label each modern African country.

The Americas: The Olmecs

The people we call Native Americans arrived in North America over 20,000 years ago. It took many centuries for these people to populate the far corners of North and South America. When Columbus and other European explorers arrived, they found many Native American tribes they considered primitive living in North America. On the other hand, Spanish Conquistadors, who arrived a few years later and explored Central and South America, discovered the great Aztec and Incan cultures, which were highly developed.

The land bridge between North and South America is called Central America. It is a land of diverse climate. There are hot and wet rain forests, and there are mountains that are cold and dry. The northern part of Central America, which includes the central and southern parts of Mexico, Guatemala, Belize, western Honduras, and El Salvador is known as **Mesoamerica**. Many important and advanced civilizations began and thrived in Mesoamerica before Europeans knew that the Americas existed. These civilizations were similar. Many built pyramids, developed a hieroglyphic type of writing, and created a very accurate calendar. They were also excellent mathematicians and astronomers. The different civilizations had similar religions and gods. Many also practiced human sacrifice.

While many cultures arose in Mesoamerica and South America, four gained such prominence that they are still studied today. They are the Olmecs, Mayas, Aztecs, and Incas. The Olmec Civilization developed around 1200 B.C. along the southern Gulf coast of Mexico. The Mayan Civilization developed in the Yucatán Peninsula, Guatemala, and western Honduras. It lasted from 1000 B.C. until A.D. 900. The Aztec Civilization developed in the town of Tenochtitlán, which is now Mexico City. It lasted from the 1200s until the 1500s. The Inca Civilization developed in the Andes Mountains of South America. It lasted from about 1100 until 1532.

One of the first civilizations in Mesoamerica was called the Olmec Civilization. Mesoamerica is not the same as Central America. It is an area that begins around Vera Cruz and extends to Honduras. In Mesoamerica, there is a wide variety of altitudes, rainfalls, and climates. Some areas are so arid they are described as deserts; others are so lush and receive so much precipitation they can be called rain forests. It was within this diverse area that the Olmec Civilization had its origin.

The Olmec civilization developed around 1200 B.C. along the southern Gulf coast of Mexico and began with the discovery of how to grow corn. It was an agricultural society that gradually evolved as a number of small settlements, each built around an Olmec temple. These settlements grew into cities, and over time, the Olmec Culture dominated the Mexican lowland. The civilization lasted until about 100 B.C. The influence of the Olmec civilization reached from the Gulf coast to the central highlands in Mexico and southeast along the Pacific coast to El Salvador.

The Olmecs were very religious. They built large temples, monuments, and pyramids to honor their gods and leaders. The Olmecs were noted for the huge carved stone heads they made. Two things make these carved stone heads remarkable. First, the Olmecs were a stone-age people, so carving the stone heads must have been very difficult. Second, since no Native American culture used the wheel for transportation, how they transported these 40-ton carvings is a mystery. Did they use rafts? Did they use sledges like the Egyptians? Did they devise some other method?

Other Olmec achievements include stone pavements, drainage systems, a counting system, and the first calendar in the Americas. Their greatest achievement, though, may well be the influence they had on later civilizations. Many Mesoamerican civilizations can be traced to the Olmec, which dissolved about 100 B.C.

Name: _____   Date: _____

Olmec Civilization Crossword Puzzle

Use the clues below to complete the puzzle about the Olmec Civilization.

ACROSS

1. The _____ in Central America ranges from hot and wet to cold and dry.
5. The Olmecs discovered how to grow this.
7. One of the first civilizations in Mesoamerica
8. The Olmecs left behind many 40-ton carved stone _____.
10. The Olmecs developed the first one of these in the Americas.
12. The Olmec Civilization developed along the southern _____ coast of Mexico.
13. The Olmec Culture dominated the Mexican _____.
14. The Spanish _____ found highly-developed civilizations in Central and South America.

DOWN

1. The land bridge between North and South America (two words)
2. An area that includes the central and southern parts of Mexico, Guatemala, Belize, western Honduras, and El Salvadore
3. The Olmecs built large temples, monuments, and _____ to honor their gods and leaders.
4. The Olmecs had a great deal of _____ on later civilizations.
6. Each Olmec settlement was built around a _____.
9. Since the Olmecs had no metal tools for carving, they were considered _____. (hyphenated word)
11. The Olmec Civilization reached to the _____ coast of El Salvador.

The Mayas

One of the most highly-developed of the early civilizations in Mesoamerica was the Mayas. The Mayan Civilization developed east of the Olmec Civilization in the tropical rain forest in the Yucatán, Guatemala, and western Honduras. It lasted from 1000 B.C. until A.D. 900 and reached its peak about A.D. 300. Most of the Mayas were farmers who grew cotton, corn, and squash and lived in small villages. They built large ceremonial centers with palaces and large pyramids.

The Mayas were an intelligent people who developed a complex hieroglyphic writing system. They also created an advanced system of mathematics that many feel was superior to that of the Europeans. In fact, their knowledge of mathematics enabled them to accurately predict solar eclipses. They also gained an advanced understanding of astronomy from studying the stars, planets, sun, and moon. With their knowledge of astronomy and mathematics, they were able to develop a solar calendar that was 365 days in length. The Mayan calendar was more accurate than the Gregorian calendar. The Gregorian calendar, developed by Pope Gregory XIII and astronomer Christopher Clavius in 1582, was so accurate, it was adopted by every western country as well as China, Japan, and Egypt. The Mayas used their solar calendar to plant and harvest their crops. They also developed a second calendar, 260 days in length, to mark their religious ceremonies.

The Mayas were also artists who created sculptures, pottery, monuments, and buildings. The most impressive of their structures were the pyramids, many of which still stand today. The pyramids were 200 feet high and made of stone blocks joined with mortar made of lime. Although some compare the Mayan pyramids to the Egyptian pyramids, they were different in many ways. Egyptian pyramids were primarily built to be tombs. Inside were passageways leading to a chamber that held the mummies and the treasures of deceased royalty.

Mayan pyramids, on the other hand, were primarily temples. They often had a base of rubble and were sometimes enlarged at a later date. If you were to take a Mayan pyramid apart, you might find several smaller pyramids inside. The Mayan understanding of astronomy enabled the Mayans to build their pyramids with the bases facing north and south. The exterior of Mayan pyramids had staircases that began at the base and rose to the temple chamber at the top.

Mayan buildings were not restricted to temples and pyramids. They also built ball courts in every large city. Young Mayas, covered with padding, used these courts to play a game with a rubber ball. This was a ceremonial game and was not unique to the Mayas. Other civilizations in Mesoamerica and South America also played the same game on similar courts.

What caused the Mayan civilization to end in A.D. 900 is unclear. The people appear to have just left their villages. Buildings under construction were left unfinished. For whatever reason, their cities and palaces were abandoned, and the rain forest swallowed what was left of this once magnificent civilization.

MAYAN EMPIRE AT A GLANCE

WHERE: In the Yucatán, Guatemala, and western Honduras

WHEN: 1000 B.C.–A.D. 900

ACHIEVEMENTS:

- Created many sculptures, paintings, and carvings of stone, jade, and turquoise
- Expert builders who built huge pyramids
- Developed a complex hieroglyphic writing system
- Developed a system of mathematics that many feel was superior to the mathematics developed by the Europeans
- Had an advanced understanding of astronomy
- Developed a solar calendar 365 days in length that was more accurate than the Gregorian calendar

---

Name: _____ Date: _____

Mayan Civilization Quiz

Fill in the follwing sentences with the appropriate word or words.

1. The Mayas built large ceremonial centers with palaces and large _____.

2. The Mayas developed a _____ calendar that was 365 days in length.

3. The Mayas developed a complex _____ writing system.

4. Mayan pyramids had bases that were aligned facing _____ and _____.

5. Most of the Mayas were farmers who lived in small _____ .

6. The Mayas developed an advanced system of _____ many feel was superior to the kind developed by the Europeans.

7. The Mayan Civilization developed east of the _____ Civilization.

8. The stone blocks of Mayan pyramids were joined with mortar made of _____.

9. The Mayan calendar was more accurate than the _____ calendar.

10. Mathematics enabled Mayans to accurately predict solar _____.

11. The Mayan Civilization was one of the most highly-developed of the early _____ civilizations.

12. The Gregorian calendar was developed by Pope Gregory XIII and an _____.

13. The Mayan Civilization developed in the tropical _____ in the Yucatán, Guatemala, and western Honduras.

14. The Mayas had an _____ understanding of astronomy.

15. The Mayas used their solar calendar to _____ and _____ crops.

16. The Mayas also developed a 260-day calendar to mark _____ ceremonies.

17. Many Mayan _____ are still standing today.

18. Mayan pyramids were primarily used as _____.

19. Mayas were _____ who created sculptures, pottery, and buildings.

20. Egyptians pyramids were primarily built to be _____ .

21. Mayan pyramids and _____ pyramids were different in many ways.

22. Young Mayas played a game with a _____ ball.

23. Mayan pyramids had staircases that began at the base and rose to the temple _____ at the top.

24. Mayan pyramids were sometimes _____ at a later date.

25. Mayan pyramids often had a base of _____.

Name: _____   Date: _____

Creating Hieroglyphics

The Mayas, Egyptians, and other ancient cultures drew pictures to represent ideas or numbers. The pictures they drew are called **pictographs** or **pictograms**. The writing systems they developed based on these pictures are called **hieroglyphics**. Hieroglyphic writing combines symbols that represent ideas, syllables, and sounds into glyphs. These glyphs were used to keep records, transact business, and record history.

Since drawing detailed pictures takes time, writers or **scribes**, as they were called in some cultures, would speed up the process of writing by eliminating some of the details of the glyphs. This process continued so that over a period of time, the glyph became a few simple lines, and it was hard to determine what the original glyph or picture looked like.

Here is an example of how a glyph began as a picture and was simplified into cursive forms over time. The example was created for this exercise only and cannot be found in ancient Mayan, Egyptian, or other hieroglyphic writing. Here is the way the glyph for hunting *might* have been created.

ORIGINAL GLYPH FOR HUNTING	STYLIZED GLYPH FOR HUNTING	FINAL CURSIVE FOR HUNTING

Now it is your turn to create a glyph.
1. Choose an object, event, or an action that is important in your life.
2. Draw a picture of this object, event, or action, and place it under the phrase, "Original Glyph."
3. Draw a stylized picture of the glyph leaving out some of the details, and place it under the phrase, "Stylized Glyph."
4. Draw an abstract version of the glyph with just a few lines, and place it under the phrase, "Final Cursive."

ORIGINAL GLYPH	STYLIZED GLYPH	FINAL CURSIVE

The Aztecs

The Aztecs originally were a small, nomadic tribe in Mesoamerica. The Aztecs had come from the north and spent several years wandering around the Mexican Valley. Sometime during the 13th century they stopped their wandering on the border of Lake Texcoco when they saw an eagle sitting on the stem of a prickly pear. The eagle was holding a snake in his claws, and his wings were open to the sun. The Aztecs thought this was an omen from the gods telling them this was where they should settle. They drained swamps and built artificial islands to make gardens. They founded the town of Tenochtitlán, which is now Mexico City.

During the 15th century, the Aztecs expanded their empire by conquering several tribes to the south and extending their boundaries across Mesoamerica. When the Aztecs conquered a tribe, they did not burn their villages or try to destroy the tribe as other empires often did. They tried to make the conquered tribe part of the Aztec Empire. This expanded and enriched the Aztec Empire. However, those who were conquered by the Aztecs had to pay them tribute in the form of food, precious metals, jewels, textiles, pottery, decorative feathers, cocoa, rubber, and other items to support the Aztec priests and administrators of Tenochtitlán.

The conquered tribes also had to provide victims for human sacrifice. Like other Mesoamerican cultures, the Aztecs sacrificed humans to please the gods. It is estimated that 20 to 50 thousand people were sacrificed each year. Slaves or war prisoners were often chosen to be the sacrificial victims. Sometimes, Aztecs were used. It was considered an honor to be chosen to be sacrificed, and the victim felt that he or she would be granted eternal life in return for being sacrificed. The sacrificial ceremony was performed by priests at altars on top of layered pyramids. Great crowds would gather to watch the ceremony.

The Aztecs borrowed a great deal from the Mayas and other cultures. Many aspects of their religion, their scientific achievements, their calendar, building, irrigation, astronomy, mathematics, the arts, sculpture, and weaving can all be traced to earlier civilizations. While the Aztecs had the wheel, they did not use it to make vehicles. They used copper and bronze for tools but not iron or steel. Their artisans made beautiful jewelry from gold, silver, and from their alloys, but they did not have glass, plows, gunpowder, or alphabetic writing. They kept written records of their history, religious practices, and other administrative information of their empire in books called "codices," made of tree bark or leaves. Their writing was a kind of hieroglyphic.

In spite of their primitive nature, as compared to the more advanced European and Asian civilizations of the time, the Aztecs created art and architecture that were very complex and sophisticated. They were also efficient farmers who used irrigation, terracing, and fertilization in their fields. When the Spanish arrived in the 16th century, Tenochtitlán, the administrative and religious capital of the Aztec Empire, was an impressive city.

It was the arrival of the Spanish that brought an end to the Aztec Empire. Christopher Columbus reached the Caribbean in 1492. This gave the Spanish a base in Cuba and other islands. Other Spaniards, called **conquistadors**, came to this new country. The conquistadors continued their exploration in search of

AZTEC EMPIRE AT A GLANCE
WHERE: Mesoamerica
WHEN: A.D. 1200–1500
ACHIEVEMENTS:
• Created art and architecture
• Efficient farmers who used irrigation, terracing, and fertilization
• Schooling and training in martial arts was compulsory for boys
• A centralized government controlled every aspect of the Aztecs' lives

gold, land, and people to convert to Christianity. One of the Spanish conquistadors was Hernando Cortés.

Cortés landed on the Yucatán Peninsula in 1519 with 600 men. This was a small force, not nearly as many as the Aztecs had. However, as Cortés marched toward Tenochtitlán looking for gold, natives who had been conquered by the Aztecs joined him. These natives hated the Aztecs and wanted to be free of their domination. Cortés was able to get over 150,000 natives to join him.

When Cortés and his army arrived in Tenochtitlán, the Aztecs were cautious but welcomed them. The Aztec emperor, Montezuma II, gave them gold and other valuable gifts. In spite of the hospitable reception of the Aztecs, Cortés took Montezuma hostage. Montezuma was killed, supposedly by the Aztecs, and the Spanish attacked Tenochtitlán. Cortés's huge army, armed with gunpowder, armor, and horses, was too much for the Aztecs, but they continued to resist. Then Tenochtitlán became infected with smallpox, and the epidemic wiped out half of the city. Cortés seized Tenochtitlán in 1521. Within five years, Cortés had conquered all of the Aztec territories. The Aztec civilization was over. The Spanish destroyed much of Tenochtitlán and put up many new buildings. They changed the name of Tenochtitlán to Mexico City. Spanish rule soon spread throughout the newly-conquered land.

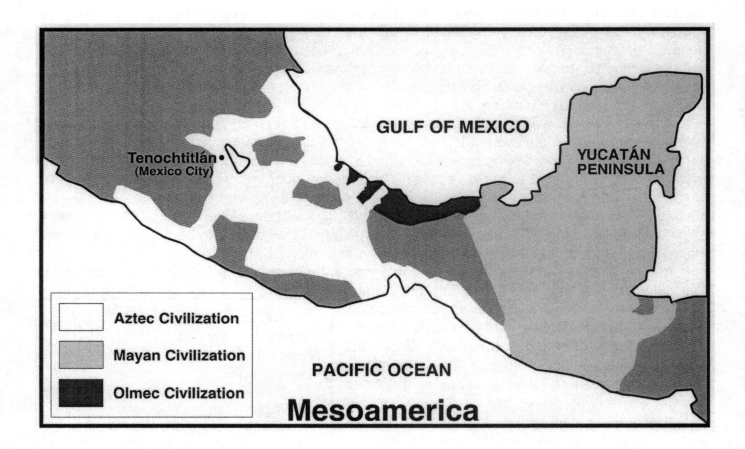

Mesoamerica

Legend:
- Aztec Civilization
- Mayan Civilization
- Olmec Civilization

Name: _____ Date: _____

Aztec Civilization Quiz

Fill in the following sentences with the appropriate word or words.

1. The Aztecs sacrificed _____ to please the gods.

2. The Aztecs borrowed a great deal from the _____ and other cultures.

3. The Aztecs settled by Lake _____.

4. It was considered an honor to be chosen to be _____ .

5. The sacrifices were performed by priests at altars on top of layered _____.

6. _____ came to the Americas for riches and to convert natives to Christianity.

7. The Spaniard who conquered the Aztecs was Hernando _____ .

8. The Aztec emperor when Cortés arrived was _____ .

9. Aztecs used _____ and _____ for tools but not iron or steel.

10. The _____ did not have glass, plows, gunpowder, or alphabetic writing.

11. Those conquered by the Aztecs had to pay them _____.

12. The arrival of the _____ brought an end to the Aztec Empire.

13. _____ or war prisoners were often chosen to be the sacrificial victims.

14. Aztec writing was a kind of _____ .

15. Aztecs created art and _____ that were very complex and sophisticated.

16. The Aztec capital, Tenochtitlán, is now named _____ .

17. The Spanish arrived in the Americas in the _____ century.

18. The Aztecs sacrificed 20 to _____ thousand people each year.

19. The Aztecs kept written records of their history, religious practices, and other administrative records of their empire in books called " _____ ."

20. Aztecs were efficient _____ who used irrigation, terracing, and fertilization.

21. Cortés's huge army was able to defeat the Aztecs because Cortés had _____, _____ , and _____.

22. It took Cortés _____ years to conquer all the Aztec territories.

23. Cortés and his men came to Tenochtitlán in search of _____.

24. Victims felt they would be granted eternal _____ in return for being sacrificed.

25. A _____ epidemic wiped out half of the city of Tenochtitlán.

The Incas

While the Aztecs and other civilizations were thriving in Mesoamerica, a unique civilization was developing in the Andes Mountains in South America. It was the largest civilization during this period, and its population was about twice that of England. This was the Inca Civilization, and it lasted from about A.D. 1400 to 1532.

The origins of the Inca Civilization are not clear. Since the Incas did not have a written language, what we know about their history before Europeans arrived is based on what the Incas told to the Spanish Conquistadors. How much of their stories are really fact and how much is a mixture of fantasy and legend is not known. It is likely that the beginnings of the Inca Civilization were quite modest. In about 1100, a small tribe settled in the Cuzco Valley in the Andes Mountains of South America. They spoke a language called Quechua. In their language, they used the word *Inca* to refer to their rulers. Today, "**Inca**" refers to their civilization. For many years, the Incan culture was very similar to other cultures in the area. They had a strong state with the city of Cuzco as its capital. However, in the late 1300s, the Incan Empire, under the leadership of Pachacuti, began to expand from the Cuzco region of the Andes Mountains.

Pachacuti Inca Yupanqui was an excellent ruler and military leader. While he reorganized the government and rebuilt the capital, he also began to attack and defeat nearby tribes. The battles of conquest were brutal invasions, and resistance was crushed. Not all of the clashes between the Incas and other neighboring tribes ended in war. Some tribes realized they were not strong enough to defeat the Incas, so they joined them and fought on their side. Eventually, the Incan army was so large that most tribes offered little resistance. As they advanced their empire, the Incas built roads and established military strongholds in order to maintain their newly-gained territory.

After about ten years, Pachacuti's son, Topa Inca Yupanqui, took over the army and continued the Incan expansion. Under Topa Yupanqui's leadership, the Incan Empire expanded along the western coast of South America and even into the rain forests. As the empire grew, the Incas required those who were conquered to accept the Incan culture. They had to learn the Quechua language and worship the Incan gods. Of course, they were also subject to the Incan laws. In order for the conquered people to learn the Incan culture, the Incas supplied teachers to instruct them in such things as how to grow crops and how to build villages the Inca way. Those who would not accept the Inca way of life either became slaves or were sent somewhere else to live. The land of those who were banished was given to those who accepted the Incan culture.

There are many comparisons between the Incas and the empires in Central America, such as the Aztecs and the Mayas. They were similar in many ways, but they were also different in other ways. Unlike the empires in Central America, the Incas did not rule the conquered tribes. They would let local rulers retain their positions if they were loyal to the Incas and if they fought on their side. Each tribe was independent and was ruled by a council of elders. The tribe was loyal to the ruler of the empire who was called the "Inca" whom they believed was descended from the sun god. While

---

INCA EMPIRE AT A GLANCE

WHERE: The Andes Mountains of South America

WHEN: A.D. 1100–1532

ACHIEVEMENTS:
- Created beautiful art
- Developed a method of counting and record keeping by using a process of tying knots in strings
- Great advances in medicine
- Built a large network of stone roads
- Expert builders who cut stones by hand and built structures without mortar

the conquered tribe became an Incan tribe, they still maintained local control. We refer to the Incan Empire, but it was more like a group of independent tribes that shared the same culture.

Some of the most notable achievements of the Incas were in the field of medicine. While the Incan view of disease could be called primitive, their treatments were remarkably effective. They believed that sickness was either a punishment from the gods or the result of evil magic. When someone was sick, the first treatment was to make a sacrifice to please the gods. They also used amulets, spells, and chants to rid the patient of evil. This often worked. We know today that a patient's confidence in his doctor and his treatment are very important in recovery.

The Incas also used herbs to treat many diseases, such as dysentery and ulcers. The use of herbs in medicine is widely accepted in the field of medicine today. One of the medicines, quinine, which the Incas used to cure fever, is used today in the treatment of malaria and heart irregularities.

The Incas also performed many medical feats that were remarkable for their time. Surgeon-priests were able to perform brain surgery and amputate limbs when needed. Prior to the surgery, the surgeons would have patients chew coca leaves in order to dull the pain. Coca is a shrub native to South America. After the surgery, the surgeon would burn or cauterize the wound to deaden the feelings and prevent infection. Then they would bite off the heads of large ants and use the jaws of the ants to clamp the wound shut. Surgeon-priests also performed blood transfusions hundreds of years before scientists in other parts of the world did. Since many Incas shared the same blood group, these transfusions were usually successful.

In the early part of the 16th century (1500s), when the Incan Empire was at its height, the Spaniards were exploring the newly-discovered Americas. Francisco Pizarro, a Spaniard who was already wealthy, was living in Panama. He had heard of how Hernando Cortés had conquered the Aztecs in 1521, and he also wanted to gain wealth and fame. Pizarro had heard of a rich empire that existed on the coast of South America. When King Charles V of Spain appointed Pizarro the governor of Peru, he took about 200 soldiers into the Andes Mountains searching for this wealthy civilization. He found the Incan Empire in turmoil. Over 250,000 Incas had died of smallpox, a disease unknown in their land before Europeans had arrived. There had also been a civil war between two brothers, Huascar and Atahualpa, both of whom wanted to become the ruler of the Incan Empire. Atahualpa had won, but the empire had been weakened.

In 1532, Pizarro marched into the Incan city called Cajarmaraca and met with Atahualpa, the new Incan leader. Since there were so few Spanish and so many Incas, Atahualpa felt he had nothing to fear. When he arrived, however, Pizarro's men attacked and massacred the Incas. This was easy to do since the Incas were unarmed, and Pizarro had cannons, muskets, steel swords and spears, and soldiers on horseback. With Atahualpa as a hostage, the Spaniards were able to loot the Incan camp.

Atahualpa offered to buy his freedom with a room full of gold. Pizarro agreed, but after the ransom arrived, Pizarro broke his promise. Instead of releasing him, he put the Incan ruler on trial. Atahualpa was charged with killing his brother, worshipping idols, and having several wives. Atahualpa was found guilty and was executed. Without a leader, the Incas were unable to organize well enough to defend themselves. Pizarro was eventually able to conquer the Incas.

Name: _____ Date: _____

Incan Civilization Quiz

Shown below are a number of sentences. Some are true and some are false. If the sentence is true, write "true" in front of the sentence. If the sentence is false, write a term that could replace the word in bold type to make the sentence true.

_____ 1. Most of what we know about the Incas before Europeans arrived is based on what they told the **French** Conquistadors.

_____ 2. In the Inca language, the word *Inca* means **godlike**.

_____ 3. The Incas spoke a language called **Incanese.**

_____ 4. Under Topa Yupanqui, the Incan empire **decreased**.

_____ 5. The Incas required those that they conquered to accept the Incan **culture**.

_____ 6. The Incan culture developed in the **Rocky** Mountains in South America.

_____ 7. Those who did not accept the Incan culture became **slaves** or were sent away.

_____ 8. The Incas did not have an **oral** language.

_____ 9. Some of the Incas' notable achievements were in the field of **poetry**.

_____ 10. The Incan Civilization was the **smallest** civilization during this period.

_____ 11. Incas believed sickness was a **message** from the gods or the result of evil magic.

_____ 12. The **land** of the banished was given to those who accepted the Incan culture.

_____ 13. The Incas used **acupuncture** to treat many diseases.

_____ 14. Incas first tried to cure someone who was sick by making a **pledge** to please the gods.

_____ 15. Atahualpa defeated his brother **Montezuma**.

_____ 16. Incas used **iodine** to cure fever. Today it is used to treat malaria.

_____ 17. Each Incan tribe was **independent** and was ruled by a council of elders.

_____ 18. The Incas did not **rule** conquered tribes, but let local loyal rulers retain their positions.

_____ 19. Over 250,000 Incas died of **influenza** before Pizarro arrived.

_____ 20. King Charles V of Spain appointed Pizarro to be the **governor** of Peru.

_____ 21. The Incan tribes believed their ruler descended from the **leopard god**.

_____ 22. Pizarro was able to **massacre** the Incas because the Incas were unarmed and Pizarro had many soldiers and weapons.

_____ 23. **Sorcerers** were able to perform brain surgery and amputate limbs.

_____ 24. Incan surgeons would use the jaws of **leeches** to clamp wounds shut.

_____ 25. Incan surgeon-priests performed blood **transfusions** hundreds of years before scientists in other parts of the world did.

Name: _____ Date: _____

Central American Map Activity

Shown below is an outline map of Central America, the home of several ancient civilizations such as the Olmecs, Mayans, and the Aztecs. Identify and label the modern Central American countries.

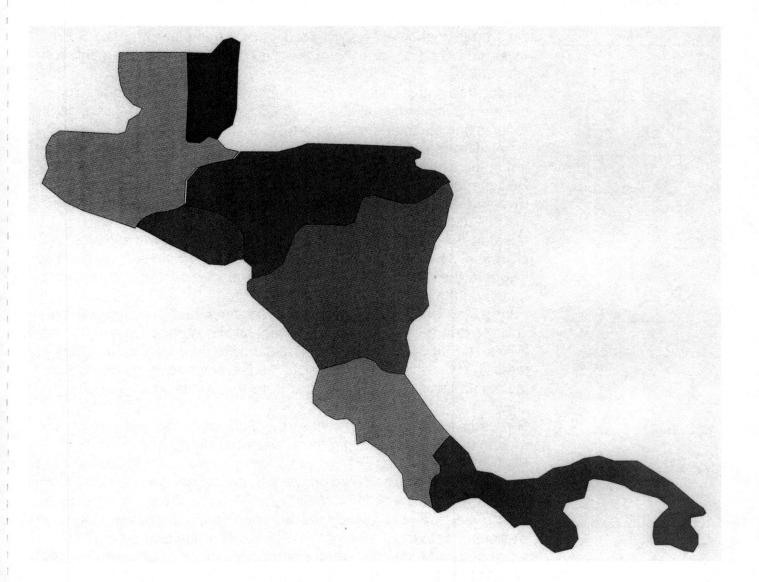

Name: _____ Date: _____

Inventions of Cultures

Much of our everyday life is influenced by ancient cultures. Their inventions, the laws they devised, and the stories they created are so much a part of our modern world we don't even realize it. Listed below are just a few of the contributions ancient civilizations have made to our present world. Match the contribution with the civilization that gave us the contribution. Write the name of the culture in front of the appropriate description. The various cultures are given below.

CIVILIZATION   **ACCOMPLISHMENT**

_____ 1. Built huge monuments such as pyramids, temples, and the Sphinx. Invented a kind of paper from the papyrus plant. Invented a calendar with 365 days.

_____ 2. Discovered and cultivated silk. Built a huge wall to protect their country. Invented gunpowder, rockets, magnetic compass, book printing, paper money, porcelain, and much more.

_____ 3. Established laws that serve as a basis for legal systems for many countries. Latin, their language, is the basis for many other languages. Built magnificent structures, such as the Colosseum and the Pantheon. Invented a numbering system and the Julian calendar, both of which are still used today. Introduced concrete and road signs.

_____ 4. Created the world's first civilization where people lived together in a city-state. They divided the year and the circle into 360 parts. They invented the plow and the sailboat. Developed a 12-month calendar based on the lunar cycles.

_____ 5. Formed the world's first democracy. Produced the first dramas and developed drama as art. Built magnificent buildings and beautiful statues. Wrote literature and poetry. Took a scientific approach to the study of medicine. Were the first to write histories. Developed a method of classifying plants. Developed rules for geometry and made other mathematical contributions.

_____ 6. Devised a code of laws, known as the *Code of Hammurabi,* which was among the first laws designed to protect the weak.

_____ 7. Believed in one God. Established a set of moral laws called the "Ten Commandments." Their religious beliefs strongly influenced many modern-day religions. Recorded their history, laws, and beliefs in the *Bible.*

_____ 8. Built huge pyramids. Developed a system of mathematics many feel was superior to the mathematics developed by the Europeans. Had an advanced understanding of astronomy. Developed a solar calendar 365 days in length that was more accurate than the Gregorian calendar.

_____ 9. Invented the alphabet and a writing system. Produced high-quality dyes and glass.

Use these words: **Babylonians, Egyptians, Greeks, Hebrews, Mayas, Phoenicians, Romans, Sumerians, Chinese**

Name: _____ Date: _____

Become an Archaeologist

A scientist who studies past civilizations is called an **archaeologist**. He or she often travels to a site where a past civilization existed and excavates the area in order to find objects produced or shaped by people of a previous civilization. These items, which are often tools, pottery, or weapons, are called **artifacts**. By studying these artifacts, archaeologists are able to infer what the past civilization was like. To **infer** or to make an **inference** simply means that the archaeologist makes a conclusion based on the artifacts discovered. Here is an example. Suppose an archaeologist is excavating a site and she finds a large number and variety of weapons. She might conclude the civilization spent much of its time at war. If agricultural items such as plows, yokes, or scythes are found, she might infer that the people were farmers.

This sounds simple enough, but it really isn't. First of all, whole or complete items are rarely found. Usually only bits and pieces of pottery, tools, or statues are uncovered. Second, the artifact may have been changed or damaged by the earth or water by being buried for so long. Third, identifying these bits and pieces is not always easy. If a piece of metal shaped like an ax is found, the archaeologist must decide if it is a tool, a weapon, or something else.

Let's see how good an archaeologist you are. Shown below are several artifacts discovered at a site. Listed with each artifact is its composition and a short description. You are to identify the artifacts and state their probable uses. Your next step is to make inferences about the civilization that used them. In other words, what do you know about the civilization based on the artifacts?

1. Silver—1 inch in diameter

_____

_____

_____

_____

2. Bronze—sharp at bottom

_____

_____

_____

_____

3. Bronze—3 inches high

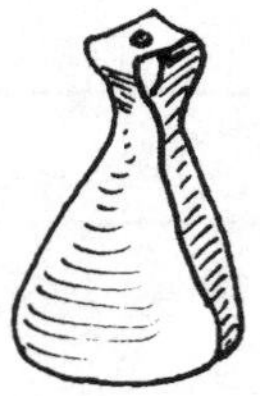

_____

_____

_____

_____

Name: _____   Date: _____

4. Terra Cotta—3 inches long   _____

_____

_____

_____

5. Bone—3 inches long   _____

_____

_____

_____

6. Polished bronze   _____

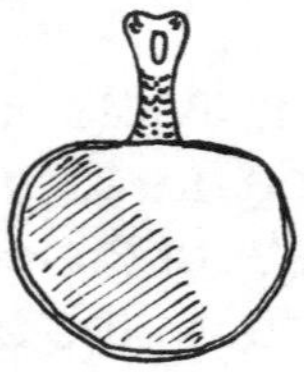

_____

_____

_____

7. Bronze—sharp on bottom   _____

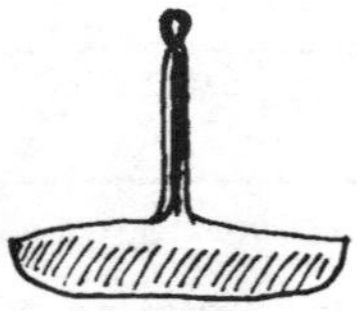

_____

_____

_____

8. Terra Cotta—length 3/4 inch   _____

_____

_____

_____

9. Stone—5 feet high   _____

_____

_____

_____

Name: _____   Date: _____

Twentieth-Century Artifacts

It is sometimes difficult for archaeologists to identify an artifact and decide how it was used by a past culture because different cultures had different traditions and values. The lifestyle of the culture being investigated may be so different from those investigating it, the artifacts may have no meaning at all. For example, an archeologist may discover a long, thin, metal object. Was it a weapon, tool, toy, or a religious object?

To show how difficult it is to determine the purpose of artifacts, look at the pictures below and identify each object. Most of the items were common in the United States within the last 100 years. A few may be a little older. After you complete the exercise, consider how difficult it must be for an archaeologist to reach a conclusion about an unknown culture by discovering only a fragment of an artifact from a culture that may be several thousands of years old.

1. _____ 2. _____ 3. _____ 4. _____

5. _____ 6. _____ 7. _____ 8. _____

9. _____ 10. _____ 11. _____ 12. _____

Name: _____ Date: _____

Modern Artifacts

This is an exercise the class can do together. Have each student bring a common, everyday item to school. Any ordinary item that can be found in the home or school will do. It can be an article of clothing, a tool, a container, a book, and so on. Place all of the items on the desk in the front of the room. Instruct the class that they are archaeologists who have just uncovered a site and found the items being displayed on the desk. These "artifacts" are from an unknown civilization, and their purpose and function are not known to the students. By analyzing the "artifacts," however, the students may be able to determine what each item is, what it was used for, and then make conclusions about the civilization based on the artifacts.

Hold up individual artifacts and have students list its characteristics: size, shape, color, and composition. Then have them brainstorm about possible uses of the artifact using the list of characteristics of the item to support their conclusions. Encourage students to be creative and consider every possible way the artifact may have been used. Here's an example: Suppose one of the artifacts is a letter opener. Some students might suggest it is a knife. Others might feel it is a sacrificial dagger used in a temple. Still others might feel it could be a tool used to plant seeds. After closer examination of the artifact's characteristics, they might realize that it is not sharp enough to be a knife, not strong enough to be a sacrificial dagger, and the wrong shape to be used for planting. The students will, if they can, rule out every use for the artifact but the correct one. Sometimes, however, precise identification may not be possible. The artifact may have more than one possible use.

After the students identify each item and decide how it was used, they should make inferences about the civilization based on the artifacts they discussed. Ask the following questions, and as each is discussed, the students' conclusions can be recorded on the board or overhead.

1. What kind of food did the people of this civilization eat?

2. What type of home did they live in?

3. What kind of clothing did they wear?

4. What was their religion?

5. What was their art like?

6. What did they do for recreation?

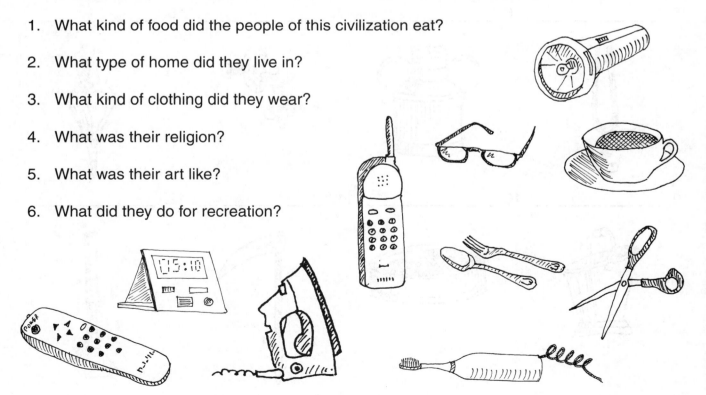

Name: _____ Date: _____

Piecing Together an Artifact

1.   Divide your students into five groups.

2.   Cut the graphic shown below along the dotted lines and give each group one of the pieces. Make sure that the groups can't show their fragments to the other groups.

3.   Explain that they are to assume they are archaeologists and have just discovered a fragment of a sculpture. Based on that one fragment, they are to decide what the original, whole sculpture looked like.

4.   Give the individual groups time to discuss what the original sculpture looked like. Then have each group draw a picture of the original sculpture based on their discussion. Collect the pictures.

5.   Have each group join another group and have them piece their two fragments together. Then have them repeat the process they have just gone through. Again, have them draw another picture based on their discussion.
     If a group that has a fragment of the top part of the sculpture joins with one that has a fragment of the bottom part of the sculpture, their resulting picture should be similar to the original. If groups that both have either top parts or bottom parts merge, their resulting picture will probably be quite different. You may want to repeat Step 5 with three groups to see if the pictures become even more accurate.

6.   Share each of the five first pictures with the class. Which is the most accurate? Share the second pictures with the class. Which are the most accurate? Share the third pictures, if the groups completed a third round of pictures. Which are the most accurate? Discuss the problems they had in completing the assignment and relate them to the problems that archaeologists have in working with artifacts.

Name: _____ Date: _____

Tips for Making a Time Capsule

Archaeologists are able to discover a great deal about an ancient civilization by excavating sites where the civilization existed and by studying the artifacts uncovered at these sites. An **artifact** is an object made or shaped by humans. Examples include tools, weapons, and objects of art. The artifacts archaeologists discover are like pieces in a gigantic jigsaw puzzle. Archaeologists try to fit these pieces together in order to learn all about the civilization they are studying. Their task is not easy. Sometimes only a few artifacts can be found. At other times, the artifacts that are found are broken or incomplete. And occasionally, the artifacts are so unusual that their purpose cannot even be determined. The archaeologist must analyze these artifacts, which represent only a small part of the civilization, and make conclusions concerning the civilization, its citizens, its religion, and the details of daily life.

If these ancient civilizations had known that future civilizations would like to know more about their cultures, they might have left more clues. Someone might have written a history of the civilization, gathered artifacts revealing the culture, sealed them in a sturdy container and buried the container so that future people could discover it and learn more about the civilization. If they had done this, they would have created a **time capsule**. A time capsule is a container filled with information and objects that reveal how life was at a particular time and place in history.

While time capsules were not used by ancient cultures, they are common today. Churches, governments, clubs, schools and even individuals create their own time capsules. It is also possible for students to make time capsules. A class can make a time capsule that includes information about and "artifacts" from their lives and their class and then decide where it can be safely stored so that it may be opened several years in the future.

Your assignment is to prepare a time capsule to be opened sometime in the future.

Step One: As a class, decide when the time capsule will be opened and by whom. You might decide to have the capsule opened on a specific date in the future. Or you might choose to have it opened on a particular occasion, such as the turn of the century or when the school is torn down and replaced, or at a class reunion. The longer the date is in the future, the more meaningful it will be to those who open it.

Step Two: Decide what to put into the time capsule. Each person in the class should choose one item to place in the capsule. The item you choose should reveal something about your current world. Be prepared to explain why you chose the item and what you specifically expect this item to reveal about your life and culture.

Here are some of the things you should consider as you make your choice.

1. Consider who will be opening the capsule and when. Obviously, if you expect it to be opened in a few years, you would not need to write a short history of our country and how our government works.

100

Name: _____ Date: _____

2. Don't choose anything that is perishable. There is a temptation to include food or similar perishable items, but not only will these items spoil and decay, they may damage other items in the capsule.

3. Include artifacts that reflect different aspects of our culture. They may include serious items, such as a copy of a newspaper, or something silly, such as a comic book.

4. Select books and documents printed on the highest quality paper you can find. Newspapers and many magazines are printed on low-quality paper that not only deteriorates quickly but also causes the deterioration of other items in the capsule. These kinds of documents may be photocopied onto high-quality paper so they will last longer. Another option is laminating the items you would like to include.

5. Photographs are great to include, but since black and white photos do not deteriorate as quickly as color prints, they make a better choice for a time capsule.

6. Choose items that do not require technology or equipment to operate. Technology changes so rapidly that if you make any kind of recording, it may not be able to be played if the time capsule is opened several years in the future. For example, if you had buried your time capsule in the early 1970s you may have decided to include an 8-track tape recording or a reel to reel video recording. It would be very difficult for anyone opening that capsule today to play these kinds of recordings. Who knows what kind of technology will be available in the future?

7. When all the items have been selected and explained, the class should decide if anything else needs to be added.

8. Include a list of predictions of what the world will be like when the capsule is opened. Each class member should provide at least one prediction.

Step 3: Choosing a container. Perhaps the most important decision you will need to make is what kind of container you will use for your time capsule. Will it be buried, placed in a wall, or just stored in a safe place? When we think of a time capsule, most people picture burying it in the ground. This is probably the *worst* way to store a time capsule. First, a time capsule stored under ground is at great risk of deteriorating and leaking, which would ruin the contents. Second, time capsules that have been buried many years in the past often cannot be found when they are scheduled to be opened. Alternatives to a time capsule buried underground are a bank box or sealed box stored in a safe location. However, if you do choose to bury a time capsule underground, pick a container that is non-rusting, leak proof, and durable. Polypropylene, aluminum, and stainless steel are good choices. You can also buy commercial time capsule products.

Name: _____ Date: _____

Step 4: Putting it together.

1. Put each item in an envelope, folder, or wrap it in acid-free tissue. Label these envelopes in pencil.

2. If you include photographs, place each one in a separate envelope or separate them with acid-free paper so they do not stick together.

3. Make two copies of a list of the contents of the time capsule. Place one copy in the capsule and file the other in a safe place.

4. Label the outside of the capsule clearly with a permanent material.

Step 5: Have a sealing ceremony where you formally christen the time capsule.

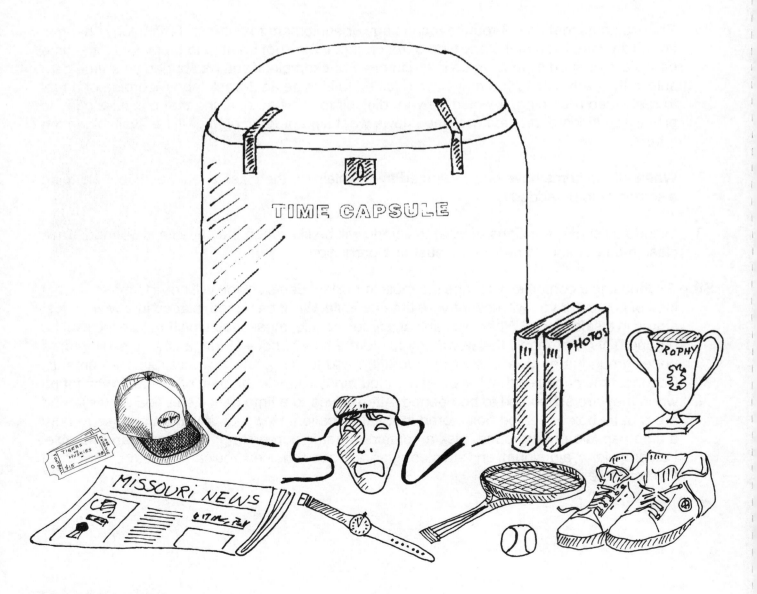

Answer Keys

Identifying Modern Countries in the Fertile Crescent (page 1)

Israel, Lebanon, Syria, Iraq, and western Iran are found in the area known as the Fertile Crescent.

Sumerian Civilization Quiz (page 5)

1. Euphrates, Tigris
2. levees and irrigation canals
3. temple-towers
4. Mesopotamia
5. Sumerians
6. Sumer
7. written language
8. between two rivers
9. pictographs
10. Scribes
11. stylus
12. cuneiform
13. records
14. ziggurat
15. city-states
16. pyramids
17. keystone
18. priests
19. arches
20. desert
21. priest-kings
22. protection
23. Akkadians
24. Akkad
25. Semitic

Babylonian Civilization Quiz (page 8)

1. religion
2. Code of Hammurabi
3. Astronomy
4. Astrology
5. Nebuchadnezzar
6. Gate of Ishtar
7. goddess
8. Amytis
9. Seven Wonders of the Ancient World
10. Persians
11. Euphrates
12. 605 B.C. to 562 B.C.
13. Hammurabi
14. Chaldean

15. eye, tooth
16. celestial bodies
17. Amorites
18. son
19. revenge
20. Sumerian

Assyrian Civilization Synonyms (page 10)

1. C
2. A
3. B
4. A
5. C
6. A
7. A
8. C
9. C
10. C
11. A
12. A
13. C
14. A
15. A
16. B
17. B
18. A
19. B
20. B
21. A
22. B
23. A

Mesopotamia Crossword Puzzle (page 13)

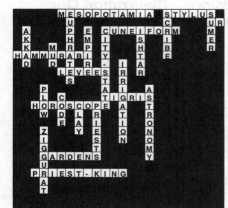

Hittite Civilization Quiz (page 15)

1. True
2. Hattusa
3. True
4. True
5. city-states
6. Labarnas'
7. Syria
8. True
9. fairest
10. True
11. True
12. True
13. Black Sea
14. Asia Minor
15. smelting
16. iron
17. True
18. wall
19. True
20. iron

Egyptian Crossword Puzzle (page 19)

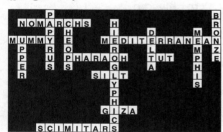

Egyptian Civilization Matching (page 20)

1. L
2. P
3. T
4. O
5. N
6. M
7. E
8. K
9. G
10. A
11. S
12. B
13. R
14. C
15. J
16. F

17. Q
18. D
19. H
20. I

Chinese Inventions and Discoveries Crossword Puzzle (page 24)

Mongol Civilization Quiz (pages 28–29)

1. mighty lord
2. True
3. True
4. Asia
5. sons
6. smart
7. True
8. excellent
9. True
10. True
11. Chinese
12. True
13. Mongol
14. Chinese
15. True
16. Temujin
17. True
18. steppes
19. Mongolian
20. expand
21. True
22. grasslands
23. True
24. True
25. True
26. China
27. prairie
28. True
29. True

30. seasons
31. Pampas
32. True
33. brutality
34. True
35. True

Indus Valley Civilization Synonyms (pages 32–33)

1. B
2. C
3. A
4. A
5. C
6. B
7. A
8. C
9. B
10. C
11. A
12. A
13. C
14. B
15. A
16. B
17. A
18. B
19. A
20. B
21. A
22. C
23. B
24. A
25. C

Minoan Civilization Quiz (page 37)

1. True
2. economic
3. palace
4. exported
5. True
6. Crete
7. Europe
8. social
9. large
10. True
11. True
12. bull-jumping
13. True
14. True
15. well
16. True

17. island
18. Mycenaeans
19. five
20. True

Greek Word Roots (page 39)

1. Drama
2. Odyssey
3. School
4. Spartan
5. Gymnasium
6. Anchor
7. Comedy
8. Tragedy
9. Poet
10. Mathematics
11. Philosophy
12. Tyrant
13. Monarch
14. Biology
15. Orchestra
16. Thespian
17. Ecology
18. Hero
19. Politics
20. Geometry
21. Grammar
22. Democracy
23. Dictator
24. Antiseptic
25. Church
26. Episode

Athens and Sparta Quiz (page 43)

1. S
2. A
3. S
4. A
5. A
6. S
7. A
8. S
9. A
10. S
11. A
12. S
13. A
14. A
15. S
16. S
17. S
18. S

19. S
20. A
21. A
22. S
23. A
24. S
25. S
26. A
27. A
28. A
29. S
30. A

Alexander the Great Quiz (page 48)

1. True
2. Aristotle
3. army
4. Macedonians
5. True
6. Greece
7. True
8. Macedonia
9. True
10. True
11. Persia
12. True
13. Thebes
14. True
15. Alexander
16. True
17. son

Etruscan Civilization Quiz (page 50)

1. True
2. Rome
3. Roman
4. Tiber
5. quadrangle
6. True
7. Mediterranean
8. wealthy
9. True
10. True
11. Greece
12. Italy
13. True
14. religious
15. True
16. True
17. True
18. Greeks

19. True
20. Romans
21. True
22. Greek
23. Tuscany
24. True
25. walls

Why Did the Descendents of Celts Leave Europe? (page 52)

1. **P**easant
2. Eur**O**pe
3. craf**T**
4. hospit**A**l
5. loo**T**
6. ir**O**n
7. **F**armer
8. w**A**rrior
9. Ro**M**an
10. dru**I**d
11. barbaria**N**
12. **CE**lt

POTATO FAMINE

Roman Civilization Vocabulary (page 56)

1. Monarch
2. Province
3. Tiber
4. Myth
5. Patrician
6. Emperor
7. Dictator
8. Romulus
9. Aristocracy
10. Plebeian
11. Tribune
12. Democracy
13. Consul
14. Aqueduct
15. Empire
16. Senate
17. Republic
18. Punic
19. Gaul
20. Assassinate
21. Barbarians
22. Carthage
23. Byzantine
24. Constantinople
25. Italy

The Calendar (page 58)

1. November
2. October
3. February
4. December
5. August
6. June
7. March
8. July
9. January
10. September
11. May
12. April

Planets and the Romans (page 59)

1. Mercury
2. Neptune
3. Mars
4. Jupiter
5. Saturn
6. Venus
7. Uranus
8. Pluto

Latin is Alive and Well and Living in America (pages 60–61)

1. bona fide
2. (lb.—libra)
3. (A.M.—ante meridiem)
4. (et al.—et alii, et alia)
5. de facto
6. persona non grata
7. nolo contendere
8. (per cent—per centum)
9. (i.e.—id est)
10. M.A. Magister Artium
11. (A.D.—anno domini)
12. corpus delicti
13. non sequitur
14. (B.A.—Baccalaureus Artium)
15. (P.M.—post meridiem)
16. (pro tem—pro tempore)
17. habeas corpus
18. ad infinitum
19. (ad lib., ad libitum)
20. M.O. modus operandi
21. et cetera
22. (per an.—per annum)
23. (e.g.—exempli gratia)
24. alter ego
25. (P.S.—post scriptum)

26. versus
27. aurora borealis
28. (R.I.P.—requiescat in pace)
29. alumnus
30. in absentia
31. status quo
32. consensus
33. ad nauseam
34. ante bellum
35. in memoriam
36. alma mater
37. caveat emptor
38. post mortem
39. vice versa
40. quid pro quo
41. cornucopia
42. subpoena
43. magna cum laude
44. addendum
45. per diem
46. per capita
47. terra firma
48. Adeste Fideles
49. data
50. curriculum

Vikings Vocabulary Quiz (page 64)

1. Berserk
2. Vikings
3. Sagas
4. Keel
5. Valhalla
6. Prow
7. Ships
8. Jarls
9. Navigate
10. Tuesday
11. Asgard
12. Odin
13. Friday
14. Tiu
15. Karls
16. Thor
17. Freya
18. Things
19. Thralls
20. Longship
21. Scandinavia
22. Berserker
23. Rudder
24. Goats
25. Saturday

Phoenicia Civilization Quiz (page 66)

1. clear
2. True
3. cities
4. royalty
5. alphabet
6. True
7. expensive
8. sound
9. pictures
10. Canaanites
11. True
12. True
13. purple men
14. True
15. Egyptians
16. Greeks
17. trading posts
18. True
19. True
20. quartz
21. sailed
22. True
23. True
24. wealthy
25. stars

Hebrews Civilization Quiz (page 68)

1. Exodus
2. True
3. Moses
4. True
5. True
6. Jerusalem
7. True
8. Mesopotamia
9. True
10. prayer
11. True
12. Israel
13. True
14. Egyptians
15. True
16. True
17. Old Testament
18. True
19. True
20. True
21. Babylonia
22. Assyria
23. True

24. Romans
25. True

Persian Civilization Quiz (page 70)

1. fifteen
2. Persian
3. Babylonians
4. Jewish, Jerusalem
5. cultures
6. Cyrus
7. fairly, kindly
8. Darius I
9. Iran
10. Iran, Afghanistan
11. European
12. tribute
13. Ahura Mazda
14. Ahriman
15. Medes
16. Fertile Cresent/Persian Gulf
17. Persia
18. Aryans
19. emperor
20. satrapies
21. satrap
22. Greeks
23. Zoroaster
24. inspector
25. Avesta
26. trade
27. Zoroastrianism
28. Alexander the Great
29. Achaemenid
30. seven

Persian Empire Map Activity (page 71)

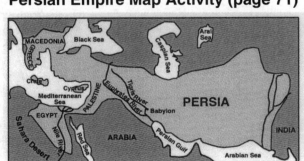

Teacher check answer to essay question.

Byzantine Empire Quiz (page 74)

1. True
2. True
3. Istanbul
4. Christianity
5. Constantine
6. Byzantium/Constantinople
7. True
8. True
9. True
10. True
11. True
12. True
13. Romans
14. Spain
15. The Bosporus
16. True
17. True
18. Constantinople
19. True
20. Turks

Muslim and Ottoman Empires Quiz (page 76)

1. Damascas
2. Allah
3. Arabs
4. Osman I
5. Muhammad
6. Turks
7. Mongols
8. Orkhan
9. caliphs
10. Ottoman
11. Islam
12. Muslim
13. Jihads
14. Sultan
15. Constantinople
16. the Conqueror
17. Persian, Byzantine
18. Turks
19. Muslims
20. taxes
21. Ottomans
22. Istanbul
23. Hagia Sophia
24. mosque
25. Byzantine

Three World Religions (page 77)

1. I
2. J
3. J C I
4. I
5. I
6. C
7. J
8. C
9. C
10. J
11. I
12. C
13. J
14. I
15. C
16. J
17. J
18. I
19. C
20. J
21. C
22. I
23. C
24. I
25. J C

African Civilizations Quiz (page 80)

1. Kush
2. Ghana
3. Zimbabwe
4. Nile
5. Zimbabwe
6. Berber
7. wall
8. iron
9. Koumbi
10. stone
11. Sahara
12. 16, 35
13. taxes
14. Mali
15. 19th
16. Africa
17. independence
18. West
19. mud-brick
20. granite
21. African
22. invaders
23. Egyptians
24. Assyrians
25. farmers
26. Salt
27. Ghana
28. Meroe
29. Sudan
30. Rivers

African Map Activity (page 81)

Teacher check

Olmec Civilization Crossword Puzzle (page 83)

Mayan Civilization Quiz (page 85)

1. pyramids
2. solar
3. hieroglyphic
4. north, south
5. villages
6. mathematics
7. Olmec
8. lime
9. Gregorian
10. eclipses
11. Mesoamerican
12. astronomer
13. rain forest
14. advanced
15. plant, harvest
16. religious
17. pyramids
18. temples
19. artists
20. tombs
21. Egyptian
22. rubber
23. chamber
24. enlarged
25. rubble

Aztec Civilization Quiz
(page 89)
1. humans
2. Mayas
3. Texcoco
4. sacrificed
5. pyramids
6. Spaniards
7. Cortés
8. Montezuma II
9. copper, bronze
10. Aztecs
11. tribute
12. Spanish
13. Slaves
14. hieroglyphics
15. architecture
16. Mexico City
17. 16th
18. 50
19. codices
20. farmers
21. gunpowder, armor, horses
22. five
23. gold
24. life
25. smallpox

Incan Civilization Quiz
(page 92)
1. Spanish
2. ruler
3. Quechua
4. expanded
5. True
6. Andes
7. True
8. written
9. medicine
10. largest
11. punishment
12. True
13. herbs
14. sacrifice
15. Huascar

16. quinine
17. True
18. True
19. smallpox
20. True
21. sun god
22. True
23. Surgeon-priests
24. ants
25. True

Central American Map
(page 93)
Teacher check

Inventions of Cultures
(page 94)
1. Egyptians
2. Chinese
3. Romans
4. Sumerians
5. Greeks
6. Babylonians
7. Hebrews
8. Mayas
9. Phoenicians

Become an Archeologist
(pages 95–96)
Teacher check inferences
1. Ring
2. Axe
3. Tweezers
4. Flute or whistle
5. Needle
6. Mirror
7. Knife
8. Ear plug
9. Statue of a god

Twentieth-Century Artifacts
(page 97)
1. Door knocker
2. Andiron
3. Stove pipe
4. Tooth extractor
5. Tuning fork
6. Milk pitcher
7. Door pull
8. Bellows
9. Coal bucket
10. Sifter
11. Scythe
12. Earth tamper